AWOL

wellspring

Copyright © 2024 TD Dierker
Published by Wellspring
An Imprint of Viident

All rights reserved.
No part of this book may be used or reproduced in any manner whatsoever without permission except in the case of brief quotations in critical articles or reviews.

ISBN: 978-1-63582-545-9 (hardcover)
ISBN: 978-1-63582-551-0 (eBook)

SPECIAL SALES

AWOL is available at special quantity discounts when purchased in bulk by corporations, organizations, and special interest groups. For information, please email hello@made4moremedia.com

Cover design by Sarah Shaefer, Design Studio 6
Interior design by Todd Detering

10 9 8 7 6 5 4 3 2 1

FIRST EDITION

Printed in the United States of America

Contents

Foreword		xiii
Introduction—Out of Your Head and Into Your Gut		1
1.	Unconsciously Incompetent	7
2.	Man Overboard	15
3.	Introducing...The Pretender	23
4.	Guilty by Association	29
5.	An Out-of-Body Experience	35
6.	Dumbing Out	41
7.	Uncomfortably Numb	47
8.	Financial DISease	53
9.	Playing with Fire	63
10.	Getting Good at Sex	69
11.	Weighing Your Insides	77
12.	Other Dead-End Roads	85
13.	The Pain That Comes for You	93
14.	The Poser Taps Out!	101
15.	Finding My Way Home	109
16.	The Dysfunction Stops with Me	117
Conclusion		129
Afterword		135
Field Notes		138
Provisions for Your Journey		145
Acknowledgements		155

One day, you will greet yourself arriving at your own front door.

80 percent of men
have been wounded...

20 percent are liars!

Dedication

For Ann Marie, my wife, for trusting me with what you treasure most and for letting me stumble along while learning to love and be loved.

For Jude, Ellie, Aidan, Annie, Hope, Jonah, and Monica, my children, for making me feel like an atomic dad despite my often falling short of the mark I set for myself as your father.

For the innumerable men who believed and invested in me long before I knew how to believe in myself.

forms with profound psychological meanings. They offer insight into what is not working in the culture and insight into what is not working in us. And the best part: Fairy tales show how to remedy our problems.

Grimm's *Donkey* is about a childless king and queen who eventually have a son, born in the form of a donkey. Literally true? No. Psychologically true? Every day. Because of negative experiences in his young life, the "boy-donkey" learns to see himself as an ass. And because of more positive experiences, he finds the way to see his deeper, "prince-born" self.

I employ a fairytale here because fairytales hold wisdom for our lives. Each of us has a fairytale, whether we know it or not, that describes our challenge to become a more fully developed person. Every tale has a turning point. And each hero or heroine, when we come to their stuck place, shows us the way out. Or, in some cases, the way in. If we understand the tale psychologically and follow the lead offered to us, we get on the path to healing and wholeness, the path home to ourselves.

After reading *AWOL*, I believe *The Donkey* is TD's tale—and also the tale of many who take the inner journey. Allow me to summarize:

The king and queen were horribly disappointed to see their donkey-son. The queen wanted to drown it, but the king was determined to raise the donkey as his son and heir. Despite hooves for hands, their son asked to learn to play the lute and became an accomplished player. Once while out walking, he came to a well. Seeing his reflection in the water, he became so distressed that he decided to go on a journey, taking his lute.

He eventually came to a kingdom that was ruled by an old king who had a beautiful daughter. When he knocked on the gate, it was not opened. So, he began to play his lute. At that, the gatekeeper ran to the king and told him of the delightful music. So, the king called for the musician. Initially laughed at by those in the court, the donkey insisted on being treated as a nobleman, so the king let the donkey sit beside his daughter where he behaved like a gentleman.

Foreword

TD Dierker is not a psychologist, but he is very psychologically astute. His book is engaging because he thinks in images and because his writing is predominantly storytelling.

You will find his imagery strikingly and wondrously clear in that way some stories touch deeply into your soul (that mysterious part you are unable to define, but you know when it is touched). That is because story and soul share the same universal language that dates back to the Stone Age: the picture-painting language of imagery and feeling.

Images conjured up, like feelings evoked, have the power to move us at a deep level, to awaken, change, and heal us. With the ingredients of a good story—imagery plus feeling—TD invites you to follow your soul where it inevitably leads home to yourself and your own front door.

As a Jungian psychoanalyst trained in Zurich, Switzerland, I have worked with adult men and women for more than thirty-five years. I am witness to the reason people overcome their resistance to enter therapy: Somewhere, deep inside, they intuitively know their lives can be better. No matter how long they have suffered from whatever is not working in their lives, by exchanging false notions about themselves and others for more true ones, they bring about more satisfying lives—where their insides and outsides match better.

It came to me while reading *AWOL* that if this book of stories were a fairytale, it would be *The Donkey*. What? Fairytales? If you think fairytales are just for kids, keep reading. They are among our oldest stories, worldwide, because they contain basic truths about human behavior. They are symbolic and fantastical story early relationships. Few escape childhood unmarked. One shame-inducing experience won't be compensated for by five trips to the amusement park. When these painful experiences imprison us in self-limiting beliefs, what's the get-out-of-jail card? Your inner prince needs to be less an ass and more a kindly king who confronts your knee-jerk attempts to run away from yourself.

We each hold the key to a meaningful life. Every life-changing story is whispering to us...wanting to be felt and heard. If a tear comes, take it as a sign that you are on holy ground. Like telescopes turned backward, tears can help us see a long way in. Reading *AWOL* and allowing TD's stories and questions to percolate inside you may help a story of your own to bubble up, and help you locate your own overlooked key.

The task is clear: Just remember. Bring the stories to light. Unravel them strand by strand, separating the gold threads woven through dysfunctional narratives. Face up to what is broken. Be curious. Ask questions without judgment. If our early lives had traumatizing moments, no doubt we built walls to hide behind or donned masks in an attempt to shield ourselves from further pain. The painful irony is that refusing to look inside is the other side of refusing to grow and change outside. Yes, change is difficult; it's hard to let go of the mask or false self. It usually works well for a while...until it doesn't. Oddly, some of us would rather die than bid our fears and illusions goodbye.

Emily Dickinson, who understood soul work, reminds us, "The sailor cannot see the north but knows the needle can." Our inner compass will always point to our North Star, but we can become distracted from checking it or, worse, feel we've lost our compass overboard. Our boat hits pain, guilt, shame, rage, or grief like hidden rocks. But if we truthfully face those parts of our stories, we can let go of the old images of who we were or how life should be and open the door to finally meet ourselves standing there... waiting. There's no more self-loving act than to welcome yourself home to yourself.

The thing that holds most men back is the misconception that

Foreword

After many days, the donkey grew sad. As the king had grown fond of him, the king offered many things to make him happy. The donkey would only accept the king's beautiful daughter as his wife, and they married. After the wedding, the king sent a servant to watch their bedroom to see that the donkey behaved himself. The servant observed the donkey take off his skin and underneath he was a handsome young man. He related this to the king, who himself observed the same the following night and stole the donkey skin away. When the young man awoke, he panicked and decided to run away. On his way out, the king confronted him, told him to stay, and offered to make him his heir. The young man accepted; and when the old king died the next year, he became king and had a glorious life.

Rejected for his differentness, made fun of, and ultimately humiliated, the boy-donkey finds safety in hiding behind a false self. He copes through negative behaviors such as stubbornness and resistance to change.

But when met with respect, patience, and appreciation, he hears the music in his own soul which opens the door to connect with his softer side and all the true riches and treasured experiences of life. He finds the courage, when confronted, not to hide or run away (go "AWOL") but throws off his false jackass mask and allows himself and others to see his handsome, unique, true self. Every story in *AWOL* is a variation on this theme.

Have you wondered how childhood shapes our adult lives and relationships? Quite simply: We do as we have been done by. Although the unconscious is a strong determining factor, the original Jungian analyst, Carl Jung, said, "I am not what happened to me; I am what I choose to become." Somewhere between these two truths is where most of us live.

One experience of shame and betrayal is all it takes in our young lives to pull some version of a donkey skin over us to hide behind.

Each of us carries a web of hidden stories that influence how we see ourselves, others, and the world. It doesn't help when we minimize or romanticize these formative years and

Foreword

keeping hurtful memories and feelings at bay protects them. Wrong. It is not the feelings that destroy us. It is what we tell ourselves about the feelings—echoing the painful story of the past—that is so self-destructive and makes us want to avoid them. And so, we spend the present fearing the past instead of coming to our own aid.

TD's book brings compassion to hurtful memories, allowing them to unfold, relax, and tell their stories. He underlines the importance of identifying that tragic AWOL-going point where one turns or hides away from self. He shows how to confront wrong or self-defeating beliefs so readers can reach a new turning point, back toward self and a more present, honest, real way of being.

Sometimes we've worn our false masks for so long, we don't know the difference between them and our true faces. But if you are committed and patient and ask the right questions, you will uncover your true self and find new freedom, passion, creativity, relatedness, joy, and meaning.

So, as you read TD's book of stories, consider his invitation: to finally accept and befriend *ourselves* in a way we may have never done before.

Prepare to be inspired as you travel with him through his reflections. Parts of his path are reminiscent of mine, so this book is not just for men. Are we not each on the same journey home?

T.S. Eliot writes, "And the end of all our exploring will be to arrive where we started and know the place [our face] for the first time." That is what deep change, metamorphosis, and a tale about an ass-turned-prince is all about.

Jan Zalla
Cincinnati, Ohio

INTRODUCTION

Out of Your Head and Into Your Gut

> "Logic makes people think; emotions make people act."
> —ALAN WEISS

Earlier in my life, I had been broken badly in some pretty important places. At some point, I gave up on myself and started believing the lies I heard and, subsequently, started telling myself. I stopped showing up authentically and, as a result, became a pretty shallow version of myself.

I have written *AWOL* primarily to share some of the psychological oxygen I was given, and for you to breathe it back into your own life. I was absent from my life for an awfully long time. I paid a high price for hiding out inside the false personas and puffed-up versions of myself. I don't want this existence for anyone; it stinks being so disconnected from your purpose.

I have long joked with my friends and family that the world doesn't need another book.

A friend admonished me by saying, "You are wrong, the world needs ten thousand more books!"

Years later, I accepted his challenge and just started writing.

Many men I know admit that their nightstands are overcrowded with books they have initially entertained reading or just toyed with. Pages are bent at page thirteen or twenty-two; dust has accumulated on the covers. Their many false starts ensure that *Lord of the Flies* will remain enshrined as the last book the average man reads from cover to cover.

It's sad because these men purchased these now barely cracked open books or were given them in order to improve themselves in some notable or necessary way. Maybe the books spoke to them, and they believed for the briefest moment that some transformative life learning might be trapped within the pages. But then they forgot about them.

I've been there myself. I don't invest my time in reading books for knowledge; rather, I read books in order to apply the knowledge and inspiration they can bring into my life. I want to find ways to improve my life, to live more intentionally. I believe we don't need more information; we just need more people living and practicing what they learn and know.

I have tried my best to keep *AWOL* short and inspiring. I speak in the first person, as it feels most comfortable and believable for me to speak from my own experiences.

It is worth mentioning that some of the impactful stories I write about involve my parents and siblings. I concede that my lookbacks might be overly dramatic to everyone else but me. I readily admit that I come from a solid and generous family with a mother and father who provided well for their eight children.

I hope the theme of this book will underscore that it's not what was said or done to us that matters; it is what we started doing and telling ourselves as a result. This admission lets almost everyone off the hook but us.

I have worked hard to understand how my early experiences have shaped the story of my own life. It keeps things real. With this as my perspective, I feel that what I am writing is accurate and on-point.

I am not a guru trying to crash into your life, looking for my cue to tell you what to do, or how to heal, or sell you a five-step formula to better become yourself. I see myself more like a beggar

Introduction

showing other good souls where to find some nourishing food that I've discovered.

The future belongs to the storytellers.
What stories are you listening to?
What stories are you telling yourself?

I love to tell and listen to powerful stories of emotional and spiritual significance.

I know of no better way to activate my emotions than to tell or listen to powerful stories. With little effort, our brains are wired to assimilate good stories and follow right along. Without obvious prompting, we plug ourselves in amid the various scenes and conjure up a variety of emotions as we go along with the story's characters in their journey. We may forget the details of the great stories, but we *don't* forget how they make us feel. At this point in my fifty-five-year journey around the solar system, I no longer sense that any one of my seven kids believe I have lived just one life. After each of my stories, they do a quick fact-check with my wife, Ann Marie. They are often trying to determine whether the story is plausible enough to be believed. They try to correlate the people, dates, locations, and other related facts to run the story to the ground. I like that they are expatriated Missourians—the "Show Me State."

Most of the personal stories I tell are not about me or my past exploits. I am actually more interested than interesting. Rather, they are about the "bigger than life" men and women I have known and been shaped by in the course of living. Admittedly, I have a freakishly high number of life experiences that involve exceptional individuals. Some of the stories echo triumph, others tragedy. All are meant to provide a lens through which you can view your own life more accurately.

Here's the first of many.

Twenty-five years ago, I met a man from Boston named Mark, who was at a crossroads in his life. He was outrageously successful in business and was on the front side of selling his growing company for more than $75 million—a number he would split equally with his long-time partner. At the time, I was traveling 200 days a year in a growing enterprise that exposed me to dozens of influential and driven individuals each week. These men were drawn to the programs and content my business partner and I were creating.

After a big event, and upon his urging, Mark and I set up a time to meet on a Saturday afternoon at his office.

Introductions and pleasantries were set aside quickly. With almost no prompting, Mark confided in me just how miserable he was physically, mentally, emotionally, and spiritually. Twenty minutes into his story, I sensed Mark was internally bankrupt on nearly every level. It turned into a three-hour-long meeting. I hurt for him. Externally, he had everything, but on the inside, he was hulled out and lifeless.

After our meeting, I was shaken up and relayed the high points of my meeting, without betraying any confidence, to a close friend and mentor. He warned me to avoid connecting on such deep levels in the future. He said that diving that deep was tricky business and normally comes with negative fallout from the person who makes themselves so vulnerable.

He was convinced that in that span of three hours, I simultaneously became Mark's favorite and most detested person on the planet. On the days he wanted to be better, he would respect me; on the days when he didn't and wanted to stay stuck, he'd resent me. The emotions that were connected to being raw and real would be supercharged with agony and ecstasy. Sadly, in Mark's case, time would prove my friend's theory correct.

Coming back from being AWOL is hard work! At times, it can feel like we aren't up to the task. It feels easier just to hit the snooze button and pretend it will be okay to punt the feelings that are nagging us to believe there must be more to life than doing and having.

It is unlikely that you and I will meet in person. Even if we do,

Introduction

it's unlikely that we'll spend three hours talking about the things that have transformed us both. Hopefully, though, after reading this book, you will feel like we have been in similar shoes. If I am effective, you will identify a shared thread that connects our life experiences in a meaningful way.

We read a lot of books, but classic books read us.

I hope that this book becomes one of your favorites, but at the same time, I know it also risks becoming the book you most despise. I believe the content is provocative and emotionally dense enough to be disarming, and most men I know aren't interested in being disarmed.

In the bathroom at my office hangs a small, framed print that highlights bits of the following story.

A large manufacturing company had sat idle for more than two days, unable to get its largest production line running. Desperate, the company's maintenance team located a retired German man who was familiar with the machine's programming and its inherent idiosyncrasies.

They flew the man in on a verbal handshake and met him the next morning at 7:00 a.m. at their largest global manufacturing plant. They conservatively estimated that each hour down was costing them $200,000.

After signing a few papers in their conference room, the visiting engineer, Ollie, was escorted to the machine's colossal, yet dormant, footprint. Scratching his chin, Ollie asked the plant engineer to cycle the power source on and off. Nothing. He asked them to reboot the computer. Still nothing. Finally, he asked for an eight-foot ladder and a rubber mallet.

Perplexed and a bit annoyed by what he viewed as old-school remedies, the lead engineer agreed. Minutes later, Ollie was up on the ladder with an industrial stethoscope in his ears. He listened intently to very faint vibrations coming from the electrical box of the machine.

He tapped a few times on the corner of the box and then on its lid. Suddenly, the line roared back to life with lights, alarms, and reactivated production zones.

Within the hour, the operations team had reassembled a skeleton crew of line workers, since their manufacturing was about to be very much in business.

All hailed Ollie, and he hung around, just in case, for the balance of the day. When they parted, the plant's engineers thanked him and asked him to be sure to send an invoice for his services. They couldn't have been more thrilled to have things back on track. They promised to keep Ollie close.

Three weeks later, they received Ollie's invoice for $10,000. There was only one line item noted, FOR SERVICES RENDERED, and the corresponding amount. Upset with what seemed like an outrageous figure, considering what little he had done while on site, the engineer demanded that Ollie itemize the invoice and provide a basis for the amount.

A week went by, and the senior engineer received the following addendum to the invoice:

Tapping your equipment with a rubber mallet: $2.00

Knowing where to tap: $9,998.00.

Once I decided I wanted to re-establish my internal connections, I was tapped by several amazing people of character and influence. Great people invested long before I showed any real signs of meriting their beliefs in me.

I have endeavored to write a book that knows where to tap—to get you back into your unique launch sequence and to resume your own production. Not so that you will be better *than* anyone else, but so that you will be better *for* yourself and everyone else.

CHAPTER 1

Unconsciously Incompetent

> "I have no idea what I am doing, but I know I'm getting pretty good at it."
> —ANDY DWYER

I wish there was an effective way to get our attention when we come up short in the important areas of our lives. Unfortunately, when you are unconsciously incompetent in some essential capacity of your life, you stink—and many times, everyone knows it but you.

Just a few years ago, my life had reached absolute bottom. I was married to a great woman, we had seven beautiful children, and we had achieved most of the things we had dreamed about in life. However, I felt cornered inside with no way out and very little mental energy left to devise a good escape plan.

I had relinquished claim to an important part of my life. I was lost in a career that paid well, but buried alive my true passions. I made some massive internal trades to reach financial goals that had been set arbitrarily for me by our culture. Some days, I wondered on the inside, "If I jumped off a bridge, whose life would pass before my eyes?" I was second-guessing myself and questioning my prospects to lay claim to my truest vocation.

Amid the pain and discontent of reinventing myself professionally,

I summarily dismissed the notion that I might actually be breaking through to what I had always longed for deep down. Instead, I was convinced that I was breaking down.

I was fairly certain that I wasn't going to make it, whatever the heck that meant. I felt like a man overboard who was trying to get his wife and children to safety. I was both paralyzed and frantic. Truth be told, I was scared out of my mind. From my internal vantage point, my future prospects felt pretty grim, and only a few people knew it.

From the outside, my life should have made perfect sense. Sadly, to me, it didn't. I knew I was better than this. I felt like a lost golf ball in the deep rough and couldn't find my way back to the first cut of fairway.

My life had suddenly become high stakes. My wife and kids were watching me and counting on me to win. Off the leaderboard, how would I respond? Would I keep fighting my way back or give up? To be honest, for nearly twenty months, I wasn't sure.

Let me explain what I was feeling with a story.

My buddy Ken is a world traveler and has had some phenomenal experiences on the road.

One time, while traveling through the Dallas airport, he was about to shuttle from one terminal to another. He entered the tram and was immediately intrigued by the three couples already on board.

Each man was at least twenty years older than his female traveling companion. To Ken, the guys possessed an air about them that testified to some prior success; the women all could have passed for modern-day Dallas Cowboy cheerleaders. Toward the end of the short ride, my friend couldn't take it anymore, so he blurted out, "Okay, I give up, who the heck are you guys?"

After an awkward pause, the guys looked at each other and then one conceded, "We are Steppenwolf." By personal experience, Ken knew these guys to be pioneers in the early days of hard rock. Ken, without thinking, probed deeper. "Where are you headed?" The guys again glanced at each other, slightly irritated

Unconsciously Incompetent

by now. The coolest-looking man of the three fessed up in a measured tone, "The Nebraska State Fair...ain't that some SH—?" These guys were obviously expecting way more from that chapter of their lives.

Honestly, so was I. My life was headed to a place that seemed far worse than the Nebraska State Fair, and it felt like there was very little I could do about it. I was paralyzed by fear and by the dark imaginings that I conjured up when I was alone.

Maybe you're there too, with very little wiggle room. In your mind's eye, maybe you imagine yourself on a crowded flight, hurdling across the second half of your life's journey. Duty and fatigue have you belted into your assigned seat.

You hear the muffled tones from your faceless pilot announcing the flight's eventual destination. You are shocked when you discover the plane is headed somewhere you had not originally dreamed for yourself. Little about where you are headed sounds enticing or fulfilling.

The timing of this wake-up call is rarely good and can leave you feeling anxious, embarrassed, and paralyzed. You might even feel trapped. You can't yet see the path that makes room for the bona fide *you* to show up going forward. Like me, you may be afraid if you come clean, you will upset the lives of those closest to you.

What happens if you flame out and crash?
Or a scarier question may be, "What if you don't?"

Many men never consider that the boredom, discontent, fear, and anxiety that they are experiencing may be coming *to rescue* them, rather than coming to do them in. The mounting list of symptoms may be colluding for their ultimate good. The discomforts are nudging them to remember who they are and what they are capable of becoming.

I have been AWOL—absent from where I should have been— for a good part of my life. I stunk at living *my* life, and only a few trusted individuals who loved me knew it.

I was seriously unplugged from myself on very deep levels. For too long, I had been ignoring the part deep inside of me that miraculously held tight to wanting an authentic life. I consistently neglected my "spider sense," the intuition I refer to as my *Inner-Knower*. All of us have been given this supernatural awareness; we only need to stop ignoring it and plug it back in so that we can listen more intently to its voice.

As I grew older, I was increasingly aware that I was tired of running. I had worn myself out trying to be someone I was not. In addition to feeling profoundly off-course, I felt like I had no good options, no plausible strategy, to get back to myself.

In that instant, I recalled the movie *Jerry McGuire*, a film about a high-energy, very successful professional sports agent. From the outside, Jerry is killing it on every level. The trouble is that he feels empty and hollow inside. He is a shell of the man he had hoped he'd become.

Early in the movie, McGuire wakes up in a posh hotel in the middle of the night with a panic attack. Dripping in a cold sweat, he's broken and lost, surrounded by false friends and true enemies. He needs to get out of this world of his own making, and he desperately wants to become his father's son again.

I had more nights like that over the span of twenty-four months than I'd like to admit. My life felt like a Jack-in-the-Box. I was the Jack—but I was also the guy winding the crank! What a clown I'd become!

I hated admitting that I felt completely broken inside. It felt weak and apologetic. I thought that being honest about wasting my life would prove to others that I was a fraud.

Maybe you are old enough to remember *The Gong Show*. It was the 70's version of *America's Got Talent*. Except in this one, there was a large cymbal and mallet in the middle of the set that was the show's ingenious version of a contestant's ejection seat.

Participants would do their level best to perform well enough to avoid being "gonged" by the host or one of three guest judges.

Unconsciously Incompetent

It was entertaining, but painful to watch. I remember thinking how humiliating it would be for contestants who got "gonged."

Many times, I have felt like I was on my own makeshift *Gong Show*, working my tail off to get through my various schticks, trying my best to avoid someone grabbing the mallet and "gonging" me. There were times when I performed well and others when I came up short. I gonged myself more times than I can remember. I wish I had realized sooner that I was better off performing for my audience of one.

Looking back, I had been AWOL since the summer of 1976. Around that time, my dad and brothers had emotionally beaten me beyond my own recognition. I was just nine years old when I stopped showing up emotionally. I concluded that leaving my rejected and real self behind was my only option for survival. I had been running, hiding, and looking over my shoulder for most of my youth and a good part of my adult life as well.

I rarely felt at home in my own body. Sadly, I had no earthly idea if the wounds would heal or if I could ever get back to the real me. Mirrors frightened me because even a glance reflected my deeper parts and reminded me of just how disconnected I was from what truly mattered to me. Internal sirens screamed out, "Fraud, fake, poser!"

Nobody heard them but me. But on my insides, they were so shrill it was sometimes hard to concentrate.

I ebbed and flowed in varying degrees of liking myself. When my outside world affirmed me, I felt pretty good. But when I came up short in school or work, I would start to panic. It looked as though I was in a modern-day Vaudeville, dancing frantically, living for the admiration and affirmation of others.

Sure, there were times when I was proud, or satisfied, or affirmed, but those good internal vibrations were ricocheting off other people's opinions of me. I lacked the ability to encourage or soothe myself from within.

As a kid and adolescent, I rarely spoke words of affirmation or positivity to myself. I just agreed with the random judgments coming from the adults in my life. The result was a rupture deep inside me.

Not surprisingly, I ran out of gas later in life. It's a terrible feeling when you realize that you need just one person to believe in you and you can't even recruit yourself. It should have been easier to raise my own hand and volunteer for that vacant position to help refuel my empty tanks.

Sadly, when we crater, we can't just make our way to the "I love myself" kiosk down at the mall for a soul recharge. Turns out that the opinions of others are like a cheap cyber currency—easily purchased but can't be redeemed for any lasting value when you need it most.

If you resonate with any of this, then your emotions are likely calling you back to the place where you first checked out. Recalling these experiences will serve your higher purpose only if you befriend them and ask them really good questions. Making room for silence and solitude is invaluable as you unpack the buried parts and listen intently for the answer. You need to listen, listen, and listen some more to what might be calling you forward toward your authentic life.

Are you content and at peace on the inside? Does your life make sense when you take a step back and peel off the surface parts? Is your dominant mental state one of positive disposition toward yourself? Are you proud of who you are becoming?

Ask yourself: "If I continue along the path I am on, what is the likelihood that I will experience peace, joy, and contentment later in my life?" When you make time for serious reflection, ponder if more of what you already have is what you need. Doubling down on the things that are not working isn't the answer for you.

More of what's not working won't work!

So many men are fixated on accomplishing, conquering, winning, acquiring, consuming, amassing, using, proving, and convincing. As if the deep hunger we are feeling on the inside can be satisfied with anything from the outside.

But the answer never comes from the outside-in, no matter how hard we try; it is always from the inside-out!

Our hearts have been designed to hold tightly to the idea that there is more to life than posing and play-acting.

Keeping it all together on the outside when our inside feels so unstable is hard work. When the weight of my costume exceeded my capacity to bear it, there was nothing left to do but surrender. Working back to authenticity is hard-fought, especially when you feel turned upside-down and depleted. I had to risk being totally real if I was going to relaunch back toward the authentic life I had abandoned long ago in my youth.

If you had asked me how I felt while being AWOL, I would have had to turn the question back on you. I had no earthly idea what I was feeling back then. I was too numbed out. Even the pain of being counterfeit no longer registered with me.

For a good part of my adult life, I rarely thought to look inside to discover what was lost and missing. When I first realized I was AWOL, it reawakened me and energized me for the journey back to the place that I had left decades before.

The realization made little sense to those closest to me, mostly because my life looked awfully good from the outside. I worked hard on my exterior fit and finish, but I was a hot rod with no engine.

When I was alone, I did not particularly care for the company I kept.

Convinced that I had to make the journey, I bundled up and limped outside into the dark night of the middle of my life. I stared deep into the emptiness of me. Despite the outward trappings of my success, I was eager to finally uncover the reason I felt so alone and discontented in my own skin.

Get Busy Living!

- Do you recall quitting or checking out on yourself as a young person?

- Will you make room in your life to answer these questions thoughtfully and without reservation?

- Are you where you want to be in life, doing what you want to be doing?

- How would your wife, children, or friends answer the previous question for you? Will you ask them and listen quietly for their answer?

- If you were to guess, how many days do you have left to live? Are you closer to the end or the beginning?

CHAPTER 2

Man Overboard

> "Many men are dead at fifty and then buried at eighty!"
> —TONY COMPOLO

To me, it seems remarkably imbalanced that we allow what we experienced in our youth to have such a deep and profound impact on how we live as adults.

Have you ever seen the movie *Saving Private Ryan*?

In the movie's opening scenes, you actually feel transported back to World War II; it's almost too much to take. At the start, the film depicts a fleet of Higgins Boats on D-Day, filled with young American soldiers, just before landing on Omaha Beach in Normandy, France. Near land, the transport ramps lower and the majority of men are gunned down by German machine guns nested high above the beach.

What I remember most from this scene is the innocence of these men. . .and their extreme vulnerability. The soldiers had no idea what was about to happen to them once they disembarked. Hell was unleashed upon them, and they were ill-equipped to defend against it.

Of the men who miraculously survived the initial onslaught, most were wandering around the beach dazed, confused, and bewildered. Despite bullets whizzing by them, they were unable to grasp the reality and gravity of the onslaught. Men seemed unable to regain enough of their senses to effectively combat the firefight that enveloped them.

This Hollywood depiction can also serve as a powerful illustration of the story of our lives as boys. When we were young, most of us were simply doing our best and shuttling across the waves of life toward the beachhead of our adulthood.

We were mostly unaware of what awaited us on just the other side of our innocence.

At some point in our boyhood, we were physically, mentally, or emotionally caught off guard. It is different for every man; many were impacted very early, some even in the pre-verbal phase of life with no real mental recollection of when they lost touch with their own Mission Control. Regardless of how attuned we were, our bodies remember; our bodies keep score. Emotional cuts leave a lasting, unconscious, or semi-conscious imprint that will eventually demand our attention.

Other men have experienced being knocked off balance later in adolescence or young adulthood. The pain and hurt can be very vivid. For some, details are easily accessed, and these impactful scenes from their youth can be recreated with ease.

Regardless of exactly when, most of us were picked off in the midst of being a kid. Through no fault of our own, we were judged, shamed, ridiculed, or even ignored while living out our innocence. Undefended in our youthfulness, we were easy, vulnerable targets.

We asked a "stupid" question, left the lights on, cried, scratched the car, sang the wrong verse, peed our pants, failed a test, revealed an irrational fear, threw an interception, scored a goal for the other team, or just expressed a legitimate childlike need.

Then, out of left field. . .BANG-SMASH-BOOM.

Someone older than us, an over-amplified authority figure,

stamped us with indelible soul-ink. Unless we were lucky, the impact encoded in us the belief that it's not that we did something wrong, but that *we were* wrong.

A cunning spiritual virus was uploaded to our near-virgin hard drive and rewrote our operating system. Like the way Christians view the impact of Christ's birth on human history, this moment became the turning point from which every experience thereafter was marked. The image we held of ourselves was now more easily sorted into two distinct categories: before we were wounded and everything after.

I call this uninvited circumstance my turning point because of its ability to pit me against me. It is helpful to view these unique incidents as though they could be plotted on a pain continuum, ranging from very mild to very severe. Although they differ in harshness from person to person, the bruises and scrapes we sustain during these moments are transformative.

It really isn't what happened to us that matters.
What matters is what we started telling ourselves
and believing about ourselves as a result.

Unbelievably, our afflictions often come from the men who are closest to us, either in relationship or proximity. The offenders are fathers, stepfathers, uncles, coaches, teachers, pastors, older brothers, bullies from school, or from down the street.

There are countless stories of how we get damaged and distanced from ourselves, each varying in severity and personal consequence. Consider these condensed real-life turning points as illustrative references:

- A good friend was accused of stealing money from his father and, despite trying, he could never regain his father's confidence in him. He stopped trusting himself with money from that point forward.
- Despite having a ton of talent and being the first at practice and the last one to leave, a friend's son was cut from the

basketball team without a good explanation. He gave up a sport he loved.

- A high school classmate was ridiculed so profusely for being overweight and clumsy that he transferred schools in the middle of his freshman year. He avoided people and crowds for the rest of his school days.
- A close relative threw in the towel on a very bright future after he woke up to find a clergyman fondling him while he was sleeping. He just couldn't make sense of the evil that seemed to be lurking in the world. He gave up on religion and blamed himself for stupidly putting himself in harm's way.
- A good friend from church was told by his dad after high school, "Be a fireman, because you aren't smart enough for college or business." After college, he spent all his best years proving his dad wrong.
- A friend's young son regularly dressed up like Luke Skywalker and pretended with his older brother that he was a Jedi. The older brother willfully played along every time. One day, the older brother had a friend over to play with after school. Later that day, when the younger boy interrupted his older brother and his friend, dressed as a Jedi, his brother said, "Grow up and quit acting like an idiot!" The boy ran to his room, crumpled up the costume, and stashed it under his bed. He never dressed like Luke Skywalker again and gave up on having an active imagination. It was too risky!
- A business colleague's father tricked his two boys into signing a document that put their personal assets at risk in his failing business. Due to the father's maleficence, all three men lost *everything*, including their homes. The boys never spoke to their father again.

Man Overboard

My own budding identity was impacted during the summer after third grade when my father told me that I ran the bases like a "fairy," just after I had hit a couple of home runs in a big game. My dad liked to call people names. It was part of the way he communicated.

None of these emotional derailments are very unique or rare. The majority of men sustain painful wounds to their spirit and psyche before the end of adolescence. If you get banged up in childhood, you aren't alone; unfortunately, it seems to be a normal part of becoming a man.

For more than thirty years now, I have half-jokingly asserted that 80 percent of men were wounded in childhood and the other 20 percent are liars. Very few of us get to adulthood unscathed emotionally.

80 percent of men have been wounded...
20 percent are liars!

Like Jason Bourne in the movie *The Bourne Identity*, most of us know we've been shot. Some of us might even remember jumping overboard. We notice that we have been floating aimlessly on the surface of our lives since taking the big jump overboard. After that, it all gets pretty fuzzy.

How about you? Can you turn back the hands of time far enough to recall when you started masking over your own painful wounding?

Before dismissing the idea that childhood experiences affect us deeply, consider the movie *Good Will Hunting*. In every one of my informal polls of men closest to me, *Good Will Hunting* makes almost every man's Top Five list of all-time favorite movies. Why is this?

It has to be more than the "How do you like them apples?" comment that Will uses to rattle the arrogant prepster after getting his attractive girlfriend's phone number. I think what appeals to us is the deeper story of triumph and self-discovery that Will undergoes with the help of Sean, his therapist. Once Will stops joking around and making fun of all the doctor's psychobabble, he is able to step into the dramatic realization that he should sober up and get real about his past and future.

"Get busy living or get busy dying" is the enduring and unspoken counsel echoing in our deepest parts.

There is nothing scarier than a young boy realizing he is unarmed physically or emotionally. As a kid, you have no other choice but to abandon yourself; it is too much to take and too scary to be you, undefended. Somewhere in this place of fear and bewilderment, I believe many men have gone AWOL on themselves. Most of the walking wounded don't even know they are emotionally limping through the best parts of life.

Unconsciously, we decided that we had better start posing as somebody else in order to guard our soft spots and stay protected from future beatdowns. It amounts to a form of soul preservation, no different from how an increased heart rate gets our motors running when we realize a nasty dog is chasing us.

We first secured our newly invented mask and then went about concealing where the emotional bullet entered. We hoped that no one would discover where the damaging round lodged. We told ourselves that if we did this well, then no one would know how close to our heart the near-lethal slug burrowed.

I rejected that hurt kid inside of me for far too long. I wasn't mature enough to know how much energy it would require to be seen as impenetrable. Unfortunately, nobody helped me make a list of the pros and cons of being real versus posing.

At the time, I had no clue what my extended charade would eventually cost me. I carefully fitted myself with the false-face I would wear throughout my adolescence and well into adulthood.

Get Busy Living!

- Spending time uncovering the moments that have imprinted your life is courageous work. Resist the urge to dismiss it or make fun of it.

- Remember that there is nothing that you are going to uncover about yourself that you haven't already experienced.

- There is no weakness in admitting that you were wounded or that you lost your way as a result of a traumatic experience.

- You won't fall apart by doing this work. On the contrary, you will become more integrated than you ever thought possible.

CHAPTER 3

Introducing...
The Pretender

> "You help people lie about who they really are so that they can pretend to be someone they are not."
>
> —RUSTY DURITZ, *THE KID*

If you are new to unearthing your past, know that it can be hard to discover when you first realized being yourself wasn't going to be safe or enough. When did you conjure up the idea that pretending to be someone else would help reverse the devastating effects of checking out on yourself?

Our memories create our beliefs; beliefs create what we think and feel; what we think and feel results in what we do and say. Our memories truly are the buried trigger to what shows up most in our lives.

I love the movie *The Kid*. It stars Bruce Willis as the high-flying and super-successful image consultant, Russ Duritz. In the movie, Big Russ comes home late one night to find an awkward, pre-adolescent boy taking up residence in his swanky Malibu bachelor pad.

As the story develops, Big Russ finally recognizes that the pudgy twelve-year-old squatter is actually his younger self, Rusty. His distressed inside "part" is showing up, encouraging him to make peace with the hurt from his past. If he takes the work seriously and welcomes the rejected part, good things will flow into his life.

It's a comedy for sure, but it has one foot firmly planted in something enduringly true and meaningful—your younger self is coming for you. It wants to redirect your active imagination back toward your turning point when you pivoted away from yourself. What a concept! If only that boy would show himself so vividly to every man, reminding each of us of where our ship ran aground and when we jumped overboard on ourselves.

The stuff I made up and believed following my own turning point amazes me. I have come to realize that it wasn't what the younger version of me heard or felt that mattered. The greater offense is what I started telling myself afterward. I traded my real self for an impostor and started building a false version of me from the outside in.

There are dozens of great books that unpack this important and uniquely male work. I point you to two important resources for me: *Wild at Heart* by John Eldridge, and *I Don't Want to Talk About It* by Terrence Real. I strongly recommend both books to any man who tries to understand what his past has to do with his present.

Statistics overwhelmingly suggest that for men who have been wounded on deep levels, most of the painful blows came from our fathers.

It is both remarkable and tragic that the blows that rewired us early in life often come from our dads. The man who was entrusted to shape and mold you into the unique individual you were meant to be often maimed you.

My own father was a freshman in college when his older brother's military plane was shot down. He was killed almost instantly over the Pacific Ocean in World War II. My dad used to tell the story of how he got the news.

He was away at college. His father wanted to tell my dad

Introducing...The Pretender

himself. Instead, wires got crossed, and the news was leaked to my dad by one of his bunkmates. He was devastated by the news; the loss was profound. There weren't the same resources available to him that are in place today. He had no way to process the pain, and neither did his family.

Even with that added perspective of something that shaped my father, I have found it to be near fruitless to try and run the "why" to ground with him. In my own journey, I am not sure figuring out why my dad bullied me even matters. I am convinced now that my father did not really mean what he said to me the way my little boy brain uploaded it.

Decades later, I asked my dad what made him think his commentary on my baserunning was useful or even valid. He didn't recall ever saying it. It was likely a throwaway comment meant to motivate me, maybe born out of his own frustration. Again, it's not what he said that mattered; it's what I started saying to myself from that point on that disabled me.

Maybe my dad was broken. Maybe he was overburdened at work and had little energy left when he returned from a long day running the rat race. Maybe he resented the attention his wife was giving to her mom and his children and not to him. Maybe he was bullied and belittled himself and never quite resolved it. Maybe he had a drinking problem. Maybe he was overwhelmed by financial concerns. Maybe he felt like he had exchanged his own life for the lives of his kids. Maybe he was jealous of the creativity and bright prospects that were ahead of his children. Maybe he was keenly aware of his own dwindling life force and its original potency slipping out of his hands.

There were innumerable things that competed for our dad's attention and distracted him from the most important role he'd ever have the chance to embrace.

My dad had rough elbows, and saying sorry did not come easily to him. I remember him fondly, now, as a good and generous man. He wanted me to thrive. I truly believe that. It took me a long time to realize that his intentions were good.

When we get down to it, does it really matter why our father, coach, or some other hero stood down and abandoned the post we needed them to hold for us? Were they even connected enough with themselves to know we were counting on them? They must not have understood that their emotional distance would leave us unarmed against the forces that were set in direct opposition to us and our futures. Sure, knowing what they were thinking might give us some solace, but it doesn't meaningfully touch the deep and unconscious places where all of this plays out.

Turns out, knowing why is just a booby prize.

In my case, I know now that my father's unrehearsed and damaging verbal assault was just an untethered monologue. In truth, it was meant to challenge me. In his own ineffective way, he was trying to offer me his brand of home-cooked fatherly advice.

My father's emotional intelligence was low, so he probably was unaware of the damaging upload that he activated in my mind that day. He wasn't paying close enough attention to my body language as my cleats grated across the gravel parking lot in my long walk of shame. Somehow, I uploaded a more complex and damaging message than was intended. I no longer believed I was potent in baseball. Later, that narrative would seep into nearly every other area of my life.

After Dad let loose, my young mind made some frightening connections. It wasn't really that I didn't run the bases right; it was that *I* wasn't right. Shame can deliver fierce deathblows. Its core strategy is to assail and mock us.

Had my father been more aware and better equipped, he could have potentially removed the broken arrow right away and addressed his unintended wounding of me at that time. That kind of awareness and sensitivity is sadly in short supply in men. I am convinced that the majority of these "scourges" are sins of omission rather than commission.

Let's face it, men seem hardcoded and preoccupied with

Introducing... The Pretender

dispensing logic and candor as if it were their kid's native language. Few pre-adolescent boys are capable of the level of introspection or self-knowledge it takes to grasp their father's message in a way that doesn't cause deep damage.

I have connected the dots now. On that fateful day, I perceived that the father I trusted to be in my corner started to leave me. Consequently, much of my teens and early twenties would be spent with us at odds with one another. I lost an important advocate that day, and in exchange, I gained a resilient opponent.

Had my father been more aware and come after me with some support later that day or week, I fantasize that the trajectory of my early life would have traced a more positive arc. He would have been there at important times to help me pivot and tweak my approaches to figure life out. He likely mustered up as much as he could, but because of his negativity and name-calling, my dad forfeited a credible place in my young life. It perfectly outlines a lose-lose scenario.

Sadly, my father being AWOL gave me a role model from which to craft my new existence. Believing I was figuratively fatherless, breaking camp, and leaving my own self was the only good strategy I felt worthy of pursuing.

Get Busy Living!

- Focus on becoming the person you trust and admire most.
- Stop worrying so much about why it happened. Instead, get your PhD in what happened.
- Be resolved to unpack your past without judgment; take out the photos and feast on your life!
- Starting now, recognize that what you tell yourself is way more important than what anyone else has told you.
- Can you let your functional adult rewrite the earlier narratives that you have long since outgrown?
- Believe that your creative genius is the same kid who fought like crazy to hold on to who he was.
- Right now, will you resolve to be your most fierce ally?

CHAPTER 4

Guilty by Association

"If you have no idea where you are going,
you will wind up someplace else."

—YOGI BERRA

As a kid, once I recognized that the most important man in my life just went AWOL, I unconsciously knew I must follow suit. After all, how could my perception of me be better than my father's? We become like the people we hang around, and looking back, I spent a lot of time with my dad.

The pressure was on. In nearly an instant, my fledgling self-concept faltered and caved in on itself. I was frightened into believing I had everything to hide, prove, and lose. Time was fleeting, and I had better get busy covering up my inadequacies.

One of the most powerful realizations for me in my journey has been recognizing the great lengths I have gone to fool myself. I had been riding a seesaw that had "Convincing Others" on one side and "Convincing Myself" on the other. Turns out that convincing others was the heavier side that dominated my seesaw's fulcrum.

To me, most men give off a strong vibe that they are pretty walled off from their own childhood. When they do recall it, they give the impression that it was idyllic and represents the best of times. Regardless, there is little doubt that our childhoods shaped us in significant ways, yet we spend a lot of time pretending that they kind of "never happened." A close friend and mentor often reminds me that, "Adults are just kids in big clothes!"

Some have been more fortunate, but the vast majority of us did not get out of childhood without being set in opposition to our authentic selves. It is sad to note that victims often become perpetrators, and the assailed often become assailants. It doesn't make sense, but it is true.

You'd think that no one would want to avoid advancing any hurt or trauma more than individuals who have been traumatized themselves. It makes no sense that they should repeat what hurt them so profoundly.

The harsh words spoken to me are nothing compared to the verbal attacks I have marshaled within me since. Left unchecked, we metabolize the offending role over time until the worst offender resides within us.

Amazingly, the hushed verbal attacks can be dismissed as elevator music. Harmless. Just an annoyance, really. We fail to recognize that we have identified with the aggressor and have spent far too much time stoning our own innocence from within. We erroneously think that we can beat the perceived weakness out of ourselves.

Unintentionally, my dad knocked me down with his shaming comments, but after that, it was me who continued to shame myself. Like some distorted "rite of passage," I followed his lead and started thumping myself with negative self-talk, self-deprecation, and loathing.

I tried to forget, but the body always remembers.
Gratefully, pain intervened.

It's unrealistic to have expected any more from the younger me. At that crucial moment, when there were only faint signs of maturity and self-concept percolating inside, I had very little

Guilty by Association

access to resources that might have stepped in to defend me. I mentioned previously that it was too scary to acknowledge how unprotected and vulnerable I really was.

It would be rare to find anyone who, at nine years old, knew who they were. Identity is still being formed and developed. Time and experience are still shaping us. If you are fortunate, the adult influences in your life recognize that you are very much a work in progress; consequently, they give you a wide birth to make your way toward the bigger, more confident you.

In my young mind, I made stuff up. I adopted a narrative that convinced me that I no longer had the guts to step up to the plate, hit the ball, and get around the bases in the game of life. It was impossible for me to picture myself ever hitting a home run. Instead, I would settle for a "base on balls" at every turn. Any success would necessitate someone else missing their target, since I could not rely on my own hitting.

From that day forward, across every known aspect of my life, I stepped away from the batter's box. Every chance I could, I stood down and missed the meaningful opportunities I was given to show up and be there authentically as me. I stopped taking myself seriously. I clowned around, checked out of my studies, used people, loafed, and mostly wondered what any part of my shrinking life had to do with anything meaningful or enduring.

I became fixated on what others thought about me. The social mirror ruled me and reoriented my entire decision-making matrix. I longed to be considered cool, strong, and successful.

I was fumbling around inside the "cockpit" of my own airplane; I had no destination in mind and no GPS to track my progress. Blindly, and without any training, I pulled innumerable knobs, levers, and switches hoping they would create lift and smooth out my ride. It's a miracle that I even survived.

Looking back, I traded in the gravity of being me for the feather-light illusion of becoming who I thought someone else wanted me to be.

As a result of my fruitless searches, I realized that costumes are get-ups we wear to convince others that we are someone we are not. Conversely, masks are disguises we slip into in order to fool ourselves.

Once I was fed up with myself, there was very little left inside, so my mask helped me conceal the ruptures. It helped protect me and allowed me to live to see another day. As odd as it sounds, I needed the mask to hide me from me.

Being AWOL felt like my internal critic was always lurking, looking for moments to catch me in the act of doing something wrong. I felt like a kid trying to switch off the light before diving into bed—as if the light or dark made the "monster" under my bed any more or less potent. What was I running from? What had me feeling like an alien inside of myself?

Put another way, I had my face pressed up against the glass of my own existence. My insides and outsides were set in opposition to one another. At any one time, most people saw me as a good guy—successful, capable, upbeat, confident, and rightly motivated.

The trouble is that you cannot upload the affirmations from the outside to reshape your self-perception. This outside-in approach fails because of the leaking sieve deep within us. If only we could "copy and paste" the outer positive into our internal self-talk with just a mouse click. Sadly, the damage is done far more easily than the effort it takes to get yourself unstuck.

I played hooky from myself in a myriad of ways. The ways I went AWOL are vast. I'll unpack several of my own gauntlet runs and the dead-end roads other men have described for me in conversation. I hope these real-life stories will stop you in your own tracks and reawaken the younger parts that you may have buried or abandoned.

Get Busy Living!

- Make more room for your story; stop numbing out on yourself.

- Go back and dive deep into your past; don't be afraid to ask for help.

- To get to know someone, you need to spend time with them. Spend some quality time with the younger parts of you.

- Activate your imagination and try to relive important parts of your past.

- Bring a pen and paper. If you just write one word, then good. It's a start.

- Choose to show up for yourself. Give yourself the positive regard you deserve, and be proud of all the ways you have fought and survived.

- Don't let yourself make fun of this process; it might be the bravest thing you will ever do.

CHAPTER 5

An Out-of-Body Experience

"It's not what you are eating,
it's what's eating you."

—RICK WARREN

One of the primary ways I went AWOL on myself as a kid was by distancing myself from how I looked physically. Maybe since I was accused of coming up short athletically, I duped myself into thinking that I was misfiring in every other physical way. When I look back at photos of myself before and after baseball, there is a marked difference. I was bleeding doubt and disappointment in every photo taken around the time of my early adolescence.

The photos of me before going AWOL showed me smiling enthusiastically with a carefree spirit and an evident brightness in my being. After, I look like an empty husk, hulled out of my earlier self. The photos illustrate just how quickly I abandoned myself. To this day, I have a picture on both my home and work desks of me at the age of nine. I am fully awake and alive; my eyes are beaming with positive energy. I feel drawn to the energy and authenticity that is captured in the shot.

Once I went AWOL, I must have found comfort in food. I grew chubby and lost contact with my own Mission Control. It was as if my personal agency was abducted, allowing for no further course corrections. That made it tough, as there was still a long journey ahead of me. I imagine there was no one at the controls of my spacecraft; I was drifting and lost.

Do this for me: Imagine yourself at the gas station. Your car is empty, and you need to fill up. Per the owner's manual, your car takes nearly thirteen gallons, but you get distracted and go way over. When you come to your senses, gas is all over the place. What a mess! What a waste of resources! How come the handle shut-off didn't sense the tank was full and stop pumping?

How many times would that have to happen for you to learn to be more careful the next time you refilled your tank? Would there be a second time? Or would you stand guard for every future fill-up? My bet is you'd never let it happen again.

Now imagine yourself at a restaurant. Are you even aware of what your optimal portion sizes are or how much fuel you need in your tank? You start ordering with the waitress, only thinking of what *sounds good*, paying no attention to what *is good*. You eat so fast, by the time your brain's "Check Stomach Light" comes on, it is too late.

But instead of the excess spilling out of the gas tank, it spreads out across your body. Before you know it, you've developed chest cleavage and look like you are about five months pregnant.

How many times does this have to happen to us before we learn to be more careful? Five hundred more times? A thousand?

For many of us, food and drink are no longer fuel. Consider, too, that the big tobacco companies who own the big food companies have us at a disadvantage. They have succeeded in making packaged foods as addictive as cigarettes.

Food is fun; it has become one of the primary ways we relax and reward ourselves. When we're AWOL, we have forgotten that *nothing* tastes as good as being fit feels.

Have you ever considered that your outsides might be a perfect reflection of what you believe is true on your insides? If your body was telling a story, what would it tell you? Is it fiction or

An Out-of-Body Experience

non-fiction? What's the genre? Is it a horror film or a romantic comedy? Is it autobiographical, or is it someone else telling your story?

I believe our bodies are the first and most accessible trailhead in the journey back to ourselves. Jan, a long-time mentor who wrote the foreword to this book, has often reminded me that, "God used to speak through burning bushes; today, He speaks to us through our symptoms." Funny how often we stop listening to what our bodies are saying to us. Rather than take our pain seriously, we disengage from the conversation completely.

We opt out of our body's urgent discourse by zoning out into a food-and-drink coma that is one part comfort and the other part escape. We come to our senses in time for the next meal, only to forget what we just learned. We spin the junk-food wheel endlessly in hopes that the false advertising delivers on its promise to really satisfy.

Your life isn't a scrimmage; you aren't on the B-Team. This is the only game you get to play.

Another friend is fond of saying, "In order for a consumer society to thrive, someone needs to be consumed." This thought awakens me. I want to eat; I don't want to be eaten. Food tastes too good these days. I don't stand a chance against the snack companies if I don't recognize the triggers that quickly bump me off course. When I shake off the cobwebs of my disconnectedness, I immediately recall that I am being hunted by comfort food. I lean forward, I listen to my surroundings, my pulse and posture change, and my survival instincts crackle to life. Sure, pizza is proof that God loves me; but my ability to moderate is proof that I love me, too.

The fact is most of us are too numbed out in our food coma or beer buzz to recognize the game is already on. We pretend we don't hear our "Inner Knower" pacing the sidelines of our lives, trying desperately to get our attention and wake our bodies up.

We'd be wise to come in from the tailgate party and come down to the field where the action is.

I have found that grace started sprinting toward me once I harnessed my physical body for my own good.

Over the years, I have uncovered a foolproof way to gauge whether or not I am feeling good about myself physically. It measures precisely how far I have moved off my own reservation.

I grab a recent big group photo in which I am pictured.

- First, I look at the image and pay attention to my very first move. I admit, I usually find myself.
- My second move is to squint and look more closely at myself. . .Egad, man! Any negative reaction confirms that I am far off my own reservation.
- Third, if I start with, "Look at that idiot! Who dressed that guy? I'm bald! I'm fat! I'm old! What a loser. I'm out of shape! I look like my dad. I look half-dead! I have a double chin!"—then it is time to intentionally reset my self-perception.

All these criticisms and harsh judgments are strong indications that I am holding myself in physical contempt.

How in the heck can anyone breathe when being choked out under so much accusation and negativity?

How we show up physically is one of the best and easiest indicators of our being a no-show when our lives call to us. It's also a surefire way to enter back into our lives. If we show up physically, we have every chance of showing up in the more subtle ways we may have abandoned ourselves without ever leaving.

Get Busy Living!

- Make time to rest.

- Let your body speak and then take notes on what you hear.

- How are you treating your body? How is it treating you?

- Movement is the oldest medicine. Just get going. Get started, no matter how small. Jog to the mailbox and walk back if necessary.

- Pay attention to what you feed your body. Is food fuel, or are you letting it sabotage you and your long-term goals?

- Break the cycle. Just for today, make intentional choices that honor and respect your body.

CHAPTER 6

Dumbing Out

> "Everyone is a genius; but if you judge a
> fish by its ability to climb a tree,
> it will live its entire life convinced
> it is stupid!"
>
> —UNKNOWN

Mental truancy is common in men. In school, we are graded on somewhat arbitrary subjects, and this can lay waste to individuals who aren't wired for or don't necessarily love reading, writing, and arithmetic.

It's important to go back and see where we unplugged from our own mental genius. Did we ever consider whether or not we could have earned a more useful diploma in the classes that mattered most to us?

As a kid, I know I said some pretty stupid things. What kid doesn't, right?

I remember playing wiffleball in the backyard with our big family. Everyone was having a turn at pitching, and my brothers were coming up with names to call their pitches. Tim threw a "booger ball," Bill threw a "fireball," Joe threw his "Yankee ball," and then it was my turn. I was pitching to my dad and said, "Here comes my F—k ball!" Time stood still. My dad's mouth gaped. My mother wailed from the kitchen window as though a Kennedy had been shot. She covered fifty yards in what seemed like four steps. She was on me like a ravenous panther, demanding to know where I heard that word. I had no recollection of where I'd heard it and had zero idea of what it meant. I was six, for the love of the Lord!

Once Mom was finished with me, I purged that word from my vocabulary for a long time.

Later that year, one Sunday afternoon while watching a Jets game, I glanced over to the table in our TV room and saw a magazine with Adolf Hitler on the cover. That scary dude looked super old to the six-year-old me, so I asked my dad, "Was Hitler the first man on earth?" Despite not intentionally trying to bring the house down, my entire family broke out into an almost uncontrollable laughter. The story was retold that night at the dinner table, bringing riotous laughter back out for a victory lap to cement my innocent miss on human ancestry.

In time, I outlived those childhood blunders. My brothers brought them up, when necessary, to try to level our various mental playing fields later in life. It was an effective tactic, up until the point when they realized it was pretty weak of them to use the six-year-old me as a human shield to fortify their own mental bunkers.

Oftentimes, going AWOL mentally feels like being hijacked by a false narrative that we hooked into many years earlier.

We question our ability to think, reason, and process information. It can be triggered in us in any number of ways. If we aren't careful, it can become so real that we almost sense a curmudgeon teacher standing over us, ready to put our stupidity on parade.

As a result of my "stinking thinking," I only aimed to be slightly above average in grade school and high school. I didn't want to get C's, but wasn't hunting for A's either. I wanted to be with the bigger, uncelebrated packs. It felt safer there.

I didn't want to be singled out, noticed, selected, called on, asked to speak, or chosen to lead. I had unknowingly cinched myself to a tiny merry-go-round and tried to convince myself that going around and around in circles, looking at someone else's

Dumbing Out

rear end, was what I was made for.

I was most comfortable just blending in. I shirked around in the classroom shadows, but secretly I was hoping that somebody would notice that I had clipped my own wings. I was in no-man's land with no fixed point on which to align myself. I had taken up residence on a nameless cul-de-sac, which is a fancy way of saying DEAD END.

I was locked into the narrative that I wasn't smart. I used to joke that I wanted to be in the bottom half of the class that made the top half of the class possible. I made up funny stories about how I got a 36 on the ACT until my dad revealed that the number actually represented my SAT score. What I focused on became my truth, and I continually fostered the reputation I had carved out for myself years before.

By college, I started to question these tattered and ill-fitting distortions of my mental aptitude. A few really great professors must have seen something because they challenged me without being demeaning or grilling me. They made learning attractive and got me engaged in the process of investing in my own education and personal development.

These beautiful people set my academic wheels in motion. I started becoming the student I never dreamt I could be. I was off and running. By the end of my sophomore year, I was on an academic scholarship at a fairly prestigious private university. My family was surprised, and my friends were mildly suspicious.

I discovered a part of me that had been shelved as a kid. I remembered how to trust my brain's ability to upload and process information. I stopped choosing answers that I thought someone wanted to hear and instead came to rely on my mind's ability to grind out an answer for myself. It felt like I was back in my own skin, mentally. I let myself be curious.

As the years passed, I realized more great stuff about my mental capacity. I discovered that there is a whole lot more to being smart than regurgitating the profundities of others. Thankfully, the distinction was made for me between an Intelligence Quotient

(IQ) and an Emotional Quotient (EQ)—I learned that there are book smarts and people smarts. When I fly, I always say a silent prayer that my pilot has a high IQ. When I go to confession, I always say a silent prayer that the priest has a high EQ. Neither is better, both are valuable.

My first real job after college was to fundraise for my high school. It was a well-respected, 150-year-old private institution known for pumping out captains of industry and business moguls. I marveled at certain alumni who had amassed incredible wealth. The wildly successful guys were almost *never* valedictorians of the class. Many of them were actually viewed in high school by teachers and peers alike as below-average students.

Recollections of these guys vacillated somewhere between their being class clowns or vaguely recalled locker partners in the halls of the same high school. What I heard at the twenty-five-year reunions became a well-worn refrain: "Man, who would have seen that coming? Nobody knew that such and such even existed. He barely made it to graduation!"

Too many times for me to recall, these men turned out to be the ones sending their regrets to the reunion committee from Tuscany along with a $25,000 check to pay for the entire party.

One guy, in particular, stands out. His life story is hard to believe and so much fun to tell. He has become a close friend, and I know his story personally. This special guy—let's call him Joe—graduated from high school and college and passed one part of the CPA exam. After graduation, he signed on with what was then known as a Big Eight accounting firm.

One day, while in the office, Joe was approached by one of the firm's partners to write a report on an audit. In their meeting the day before, this partner noted something not quite right about Joe and wanted to lean into his hunch. He brought in a short letter he had just written to a large client and asked Joe to read it out loud for tone and content. Joe laughed and said, "I am not going to read it. . .you don't need my help." He continued to stammer and cajole, but the partner was not going to be denied the evidence he

Dumbing Out

earnestly sought. He urged him again to read the letter. Alas, the jig was up. Joe was entirely unable to read. He was functionally illiterate, and now everyone would know.

You can ask, "How'd that happen? How could a guy graduate from high school or college without knowing how to read?" Or you could wonder, "What kind of genius can achieve that level of success without knowing how to read?" What kind of freakish superpowers would you have to hone or possess to pull that charade off for that long?

Can you imagine the relief Joe felt when he was finally found out? To the partner's credit, the firm worked with Joe as he retooled. They sent him to the Evelyn Wood Reading School where he spent half a year with second graders learning how to read. Stories this good you just can't make up.

His forced liberation allowed Joe to begin again. Financially, he is a savant. Almost everything he has pursued or touched has turned into highly successful enterprises. All along the way, he groomed his inadequacies into advantages by cultivating good thoughts that he whispered to himself. He never again hid from whom he was and finally trusted firmly in his own mental resiliency.

How many men know that, despite being fishes, they opted for dry land—not knowing that they would no longer be able to swim, or jump, or splash? In adapting to dry land, most men ignore their genius and end up living the balance of their lives convinced that they are stupid.

Get Busy Living!

- Stop believing the earlier stuff you made up about your mental aptitude.

- When do you last recall getting lost in something that caught, and then kept, your attention? Find ways to do more of that!

- What ignites your curiosity?

- What book are you reading besides this one? What parts of you are being challenged and stretched?

- Fight for ways to unleash and leverage your genius.

- Don't settle for scoring in a game that you don't even like playing in order to make a living. Instead, endeavor to make a life!

CHAPTER 7

Uncomfortably Numb

"I don't run races to see who wins. I run races to see who has the most guts."
—STEVE PREFONTAINE

Feelings don't come from my brain, they come from some place much deeper, closer to my heart than my head. My feelings are not good nor bad, they just are. It is vital to get my arms around what I am feeling.

As a young kid, I felt as if I was drinking from a fire hose when it came to learning about my emotions. Like you, I moved from very basic emotions to more complex ones as I matured.

My earliest recollections are of feeling loved, happy, excited, bored, worried, disappointed, and scared. As I got older, I recall feeling pride, contentment, desire, empathy, resentment, joy, resolve, disappointment, sadness, insecurity, and unbridled fear. Knowing how to feel and express emotions is dramatically important if we intend to be in healthy relationship with ourselves and with others.

As young people, we can often feel ashamed of what we are feeling. Think about it: We are bumping into adults all day long at home, school, practice, church, and countless other places. In life, the people surrounding us have agendas and things they are trying to accomplish in their days. This striving can leave little room to ask how we are feeling. Heck, they likely have little idea of what they are feeling, so why would they leave any room to ask about us, much less listen for the answer?

If we aren't careful, we can unknowingly position ourselves to become impenetrable on the outsides so that nobody can hurt our insides. The bummer with this strategy is that it reinforces a one-dimensional approach to our experiences of life. We become sealed off, one crayon versus a box of sixty-four.

People have to slow everything way the heck down to get a firm grasp on what they are feeling at any point in time. Most folks aren't willing, or able, to make the time it takes to dive beneath their "doing and having" modality. For instance, did you know that anger is almost ALWAYS the second emotion? What is the emotion that precedes us feeling angry? If we aren't curious enough to dig in while it is actually happening, then we are almost sure to miss it.

Do you ever listen to people when you ask them how they are doing these days? Nine out of ten times, this is the answer I get in one form or another: "I'm busy. You know, there is a lot going on." Answers like that one have literally zero to do with *how* someone is doing. Sure, it is answering a question, but not the one that I asked.

I have tried to make room for introspection in my adult life, to stop and ask myself what I am feeling at various times of my day. Even now, it can be hard to identify my feelings. At the outset, the "shoulds" get in my way. This is when my rational brain jumps in and starts calling the shots, telling me all the things I *should* feel, at various times and in certain situations.

My feelings are important indicators for me if I am wise enough to heed their counsel.

Slowing down is imperative. With practice, I have grown to trust my feelings and let them join me as part of my decision-making process. I am healthier when they inform and influence me. I confess, when they rule me, they inevitably wreck me. Therefore, I want to be more of a hybrid, switching effortlessly between running on my intellect and emotions.

On my good days, I can sift and scan through my inner monologue and listen to what it says about how I am feeling. If I can tune in, then it provides strong clues pointing to what I am experiencing on the inside. Curiosity and inquisitiveness are the best ways I can spelunk for what I am really feeling. I may always be a newbie at this, but at the most basic level, the exercise has two parts: 1) Determining what it is I am really feeling and 2) Expressing my emotions in healthy ways to myself or someone else.

Two powerful forces stand opposed to uncovering our true emotions as kids and adults. The first is that we are not given permission to actually feel what we are feeling. Instead, we are told what we are or should be feeling. This confuses us and sets us up to doubt our emotions as we grow older. The second barrier is that we haven't really been taught how to feel, as it likely wasn't modeled for us.

In the land of the blind, the one-eyed man is king. The busy adults who taught me were time-starved; as a result, they modeled ineffective ways to value and understand emotions. I mostly just guessed at what I was feeling and, consequently, fumbled to express my true self. My feelings were hard to access, so I stopped trying to express them. Despite the distance from my head to my heart being a mere eighteen inches, I rarely stepped foot on the trail. Untethered and without a dependable emotional gauge, I spun off course.

Several years ago, I was at lunch with an important client of my firm. This guy was financially successful, but from the get-go, he struck me as almost impenetrable emotionally. Forty minutes into our second meeting, I better understood why.

This man, I'll call him Blake, was a gifted real-estate developer and home builder. Materially, he wanted for nothing. He was mildly aware emotionally but had long ago exited the place inside him that was going to feel anything legitimately heart centered. At fifty-five, he had several ex-wives and had distanced himself from his kids in every measurable way, except financially.

He had a 60,000-watt persona. I was certain that he was the man who originally coined the phrases "Bigger is better!" and "He who dies with the most toys, wins!" Before he met me, nobody had challenged him with the thought that he who dies with the most toys *still dies*.

During our third meeting, without much warning or setup, he recounted what happened when he returned home from graduating from college. He had landed a great job in real estate development with a friendly competitor of his father's business. The week before he started work with his new employer, he went to share the exciting news with his dad. His father was unamused and asked Blake to sit tight while he made a quick phone call. Hard to fathom, but Blake's dad called the friendly competitor in front of Blake. Over the phone, he maligned his son's character and work ethic in every way imaginable. By the time the call was complete, Blake's newest employer agreed to rescind the offer and seemed grateful for the heads-up from his father about his son's flaws and character defects.

Blake was mortified and went ballistic; it was a soul-killing act of incalculable proportions. He stood up and told his father that he was now dead to him. Blake sealed off the shouting match by telling his dad that when he was dead, he'd inherit his millions and have his own fortune as well. After that, they didn't speak to each other for fifteen years. As he was retelling the story, I was struck by Blake's casual demeanor when recounting the grave emotional events with his father that day. A couple of times, I sensed he was actually chuckling.

Afterward, he looked over at me and saw my eyes marked with tears. Frankly, I was horrified by his tragic story. He was put off by my response and asked me why the heck I was crying. All I could think to say was, "Blake, I am crying because you are laughing. I am so sad about the incalculable loss of your father. It's devastating, every stinking bit of it!"

Too often, men have been misdirected in the sphere of processing their emotions. Most men have experienced some version of "emotional neglect" in their younger years. By design, they "stuff" their feelings until they become too acute to ignore.

Sadly, men who express their feelings are often viewed as weak or effeminate. This is such a disservice to men and to all the people who love them. Emotions provide a rich texture to our lives and allow us to connect with others more meaningfully as we do life together. Our emotions provide invaluable internal data points in our search for meaning and purpose, so we should follow their lead as to what we may be experiencing or thinking about ourselves. Our emotions needn't be the decision-maker, but only a fool ignores their counsel.

Have you ever played freezeout? It's an inane game my kids sometimes play in the wintertime. On really cold days, they put their windows down on the ride to school or a sporting event and see who can withstand the freezing temperatures the longest. I have come to believe that this silly sparring match is not unlike how we sometimes interact with loved ones on an emotional level.

If we aren't careful, we can also freeze others out, leaving them or us to call "uncle." It can lead to a distorted emotional game of hide-and-no-seek. In so doing, we compete to see who has the highest pain tolerance. We hide out in the most inauthentic ways and pray that someone comes to find us. Like the other ways we go AWOL, many of these emotional antics are served up unconsciously and have a misdirected intention of keeping us in control and feeling safe.

Asking ourselves what we are feeling several times across the span of the day can be like smelling salts to our emotional selves. Coming to, we can remember when we stopped feeling and begin in earnest to rediscover the more vital parts of ourselves. Hearts buoyed; we can breathe back into those atrophied parts of our emotional natures. We come to realize that expressing ourselves and putting ourselves out there with loved ones is the surest way to show them who really has the most guts.

Get Busy Living!

- Discussing what we are feeling can feel like speaking a foreign language, at first.

- Try hard *not* to minimize or judge your emotional nature. What you feel informs you of what matters most to you.

- You haven't stopped feeling; you have just stopped paying attention to what you are feeling. Start listening again.

- What are you feeling? Deep down inside of you, what are you experiencing? Give it a name, listen to its voice.

- Can you name what you are feeling right now?

- Recall that anger is nearly always the second emotion. There is a deeper feeling that triggers anger.

CHAPTER 8

Financial DISease

"Money is either your master or slave; it is NEVER your friend!"

—DAN ROLFES

I have learned over the span of five-plus decades that money represents energy. It is also a clever disguise for what I value most. When I am opposed to someone about money, I quickly remind myself that we just disagree on what we value. Money is the symptom, not the disease.

As a young man, I was not taught how money worked. This was kind of sad, seeing as my grandfather was the president of a reputable savings and loan company, and my father was really good at stretching his finances to provide a good life for our large family. Making ends meet for his family of eight required that my dad plan and strategize financially. I can attest; raising a big family requires significant financial resources.

My mom and dad rarely agreed on money matters. It was the source of continual frustration and discord at home. My mother used to toy with Dad when a notice of insufficient funds arrived in the mail. She held tightly to her innocence, joking that there was no possible way she could be overdrawn. "How could it be," she mused, "I still have checks left?"

Sometimes my dad would randomly quote my grandfather. He shared with me once that Grandpa believed there were only two things that warranted a bank loan: your home and a family vacation. Evidently, he felt both were very important and key to the healthy dynamic of a family, a cool insight into what fueled his beliefs.

Besides these rare profundities, I received no formal education in money matters at home.

They say that sarcasm rarely works; I can attest to its ineffectiveness because this was my father's go-to method for teaching. It was a shame, because he had great knowledge to share, and I had a supreme need to upload his financial body of work.

With my dad, much was taught about the need to be thrifty, but little was caught. He would try to pick fiscal sparring matches when he got home from work. We'd hear, "I see we're working for the power company again!" when a light was left burning in an empty room or a TV show was on with nobody watching. His commentary fell like barren seeds on hard-packed earth.

Teaching a young person about money is undoubtedly an uphill climb.

Save for the rare money savants who emerge at a very young age, most of us are clueless about what creates wealth. Moreover, most kids lack the ambition they need to link together the how-to and want-to of earning money. It wasn't until later in life that I really connected the dots on what Dad was inadvertently trying to instill in his children.

At one point I realized that nobody was coming for me, besides my creditors.

I'm ashamed to admit it, but his non-Socratic method left me disengaged. To me, the message wasn't attractive. I checked out and missed out on a wealth of experience.

I failed to make alliances with important forces such as the time-value of money, time *in* the market vs. timing the market, and the "Rule of 72." I woke up later in life after my circumstances waved a bright light around the parts of me that had financially gone AWOL.

The undeveloped and irresponsible parts of me must have partially thought that money *did* grow on trees. At one point during high school, I acted as though ATM stood for Anyone Takes Money. You mean the credit card I applied for on the first day at college would actually require me to pay back the bank, with interest? The government was entitled to take a good chunk of what I earned each pay period? How was that fair?

Where was I when the freaking lights went out? I spent a fair amount of time being in the dark, grasping for the basics I never learned about personal finance.

All of these misses were just small knobs on the amplifier of my financial absenteeism. Foreshadowed in my teenage years, the bigger challenges emerged later in life.

As mentioned earlier, I attended a prestigious high school. It attracted uber-wealthy families, and its students were largely the offspring of families that were great influencers in our business and medical communities. It created a virtual hothouse for material comparisons.

For example, the parking lot was dotted with luxury cars. Until high school, I had very little appreciation for the many social ranks that existed above our middle class. I thought everyone drove American cars.

But early in high school, I began to judge my insides by everyone else's outsides. I resented my father for not succumbing to the pressure we felt from looking at our image in the social mirror. Either he was oblivious to it, or he had mastered the art of not giving a rip. I surmised later it was probably a combination of both.

On the other hand, my mother was suspicious of anyone who seemed financially well-to-do or independent. Her belief system influenced me and contributed to me distancing myself from a healthy concept of money and material wealth. In my junior year of college, she retold a story that gave me a deeper understanding and appreciation for why she resented wealthy people.

With raw and real emotion, she unpacked a childhood experience that had created her own deep and abiding financial turning point. As an eighth grader, she was invited to attend, at no cost to her family, an elite academy run by an order of well-respected Catholic nuns. From the start, my mother was totally out of place there, as she came from a very different background. She discovered that her classmates were the offspring of the social elite. Mom had been raised during the Great Depression when there were four generations of her Irish-immigrant family living in the same house. Contrast that with a classmate whose father was a world-renowned cigar maker.

On a few occasions after school, she and her classmate would be escorted by chauffeur to the heiress' home. After a mock tea party or playing cards, my mother's "friend" would pull a velvet cord signaling to the butler that her snack time would commence. When the butler arrived, my mother's jaw dropped; she wondered if there would be any way she could take home some of the crustless finger sandwiches to share with her siblings.

Indeed, my mother had landed as a stranger in a strange land. Awkwardness and feelings of inferiority mounted within her. Hurtling toward the end of the school year, Mom felt homesick for her neighborhood school and childhood friends. Her intuition must have sensed what was coming.

On her graduation day, after enduring a full year of spoken and unspoken shame and ridicule, my mother was denied her diploma. She wasn't told ahead of time. She was sitting alone, embarrassed, at the end of the graduation ceremony. For no apparent reason, her name was never called; she was devastated. The now evident mean-spiritedness of the school faculty broke my mom open in that moment, proving to her once more that hurt people, hurt people!

That experience would forever define the assumptions she

Financial DISease

would make about wealthy and powerful people. With a broad brush, she painted them as mean, superficial, and unchristian. This became her turning point toward a belief that money was evil and used primarily in the killing of souls.

Although I was aware of the impact this had on my mom, it did not deter me from wanting to succeed financially. When I was graduating from college, it was my intent to go to law school. As an undergraduate, I was a waiter at a four-star restaurant. The job was awesome and allowed me to make a crazy amount of tip money. It also gave me daily glimpses into the lives of the social climbers and the social arrivers.

One night, I served a successful attorney who was part of a large dinner party. When he later learned that I was planning to attend law school, he asked if I could meet with him for twenty minutes after my shift. Despite it being mildly odd, I agreed. I am glad I did.

When we met, the first thing out of his mouth was, "Don't go to law school!" He said, "I am a lawyer, and I hate my job." He went on to say, "It's too late for me, but it's not too late for you." He related how he entered law school with the best of intentions but quickly re-routed his practice to line up with where the "real" money was. He had succeeded financially but missed converting in the ways that truly mattered. He traded his deeper passions and purpose for money, and he was lamenting the inequity of the trade.

This chance meeting impacted me deeply and my Inner Knower registered his twenty-minute soliloquy as a *direct hit*. I took notes, and my subconscious got right to work. I dropped back and punted on the idea of law school. It's amazing when you think of the influence chance meetings can have on the trajectory of our lives.

As an adult, I have strived to stand apart from my mother's experience. My journey has awakened in me my own money consciousness. I continually check in with my wife and kids to be sure we are on track.

I know that who I become is much more important than what I do for a living, or what I own. Staying focused on having enough financially is our mantra. Sure, we need to make a living, but we are more intent on making an exceptional life.

Going AWOL financially is when we fall for the false promises of money and what it will do for us.

Toward the end of writing *AWOL*, I received the following letter from a former colleague and good friend. He wrote to me personally, and it was so powerful that I decided, with his permission, to include it here. It provides real life insight into the importance of staying awake and alive in your professional pursuits. After reading it, I hope you decide you'll never give up on your dreams or deepest calling in exchange for money or power.

Dear TD,

Now knowing what you are up to these days, I thought I would share some of my most dominant thoughts around going AWOL. I am hoping that this note will encourage you to keep writing to men. You are on to something when you encourage men to instead reconsider their approach to their careers and consider the vital nature of marriage and family.

As an adult, one of the most eye-opening conclusions I have come to is my realization that a long-held belief of mine was either wrong, or way different than I had imagined earlier in life.

I grew up in a typical family that instilled in us the American dream. Work hard, sacrifice your time and effort for your employer, be the "go to" man at work, work your way through the organization, leverage your work relationships so you can make more money, be a good provider for your family. If you do this, then you will become successful, and be happy. It seemed like a fantastic plan for my life, so I bought in and chased it hard.

Financial DISease

Later in life, I had several revelations that made me question whether my real happiness, fulfillment, and success would come from betting everything on my career. As a Major in the US Army, I initially believed I was on a well-worn road to what I wanted most. That is, until I started to glimpse further into what awaited me in the future.

Being somewhat senior in rank, I frankly became surprised when attending the retirement ceremonies of Colonels who were retiring after 20-30 years of military service. These great men had achieved the highest ranks and as a result were afforded tremendous prestige, responsibility, and influence. They finished on top of the mountain. For all intents and purposes, they had made it!

But there was a painful trend emerging in these retirement ceremonies, one that I hadn't expected. These guys' families were typically in attendance along with a large number of the soldiers they had previously led. When given the chance to speak, each man expressed pride in what they had accomplished, and thanked their fellow soldiers for their support, trust, and friendship.

But you could sense a feeling of sadness as they anticipated their impending separation from a career that had literally consumed their lives. What struck me most was what invariably happened next. These strong and hardened men got teary-eyed and found it hard to speak.

Their voices cracked when they thanked their family members for the many sacrifices they had made. Two out of three shed tears as they apologized to their spouses and family for having missed so much time with them. Some even sobbed; overcome by a flood of unexpected emotions, they were unable to speak. I concluded that they realized they would have loved much better had they known then what they knew now.

These were good men, strong men, and great leaders. I respected the heck out of them. Yet it was clear they were coming to the sudden realization that they had paid an incalculable price for their professional success. A success that was now speeding into their rearview mirror. Their former rank would be unable to sustain them in any meaningful way going forward.

Their families had also paid the high price of a husband, or a father, who had traded time with them to achieve these brief moments at the top of their professional careers. With their military achievement waning and their time and attention already having been diverted from their family, reality set in.

In at least half of these cases, their marriages had atrophied, and their children were grown. There was no chance to spend more time with their kids as a family unit. Rebuilding a neglected marriage is a tall order; it is hard to snap your fingers and change important relationships that you passed over for three decades or more.

It is likely a terrifying day when a man realizes he spent his life pursuing a path that never delivered the lasting sense of self-worth and happiness it promised. Add to the emotional mix that men aren't good at admitting big mistakes, especially when it is too late to recover what was lost.

We are told that men can find lasting fulfillment in their work. I believe this can be true for men in the early stages of climbing the corporate ladder. Maybe it is actually true for the ones who make it to the very top, I have never been there so I wouldn't know. But let's be honest, most of us won't make it to the very top. What then?

Let me close with this TD. I have been to a lot of funerals. Unless it was a tragic accident, early in life, former bosses seldom attend the funerals of employees, and I have never seen one cry.

Men need to spend their best years and most sincere efforts with people who will cry at their funerals.

Good luck in your endeavors and keep in touch.

Fondly,
Ken

Financial DISease

Wow—what a letter; what a heavy weight this letter carries! I see it as equal parts absolution and indictment. Career pursuits are necessary and admirable, but not at the expense of the things that have the chance to endure and outlive us. Who we become, as a result of the work we do, is what deserves our sustained effort and focus.

In my professional life, I have spent a considerable amount of time with very wealthy individuals and their families. Some of these individuals are billionaires a few times over. Many of these people have earned their fortunes. Others have inherited wealth, and some others have married into a much higher tax bracket. I have marveled at the various ways money has impacted these people. There are some similarities woven into each of their stories.

My attorney friends will testify that it is a rarity to see a man or family that amassed excessive amounts of money that didn't handicap most everyone close to them. Fear, resentment, entitlement, lethargy, addiction, dishonesty, insecurity, materialism, and broken relationships are standard outcomes for individuals who make power and riches their sole focus. If you are not careful, when you succeed, you'll win false friends and betray those who matter most.

I was recently convicted by this enduring maxim: "Power and money don't ruin a person's character; they reveal it!"

Get Busy Living!

- Recognize that money is a terrible way to get your emotional needs met.

- Money is overrated. We lose a big part of ourselves in the pursuit of it, so why not align your energy and life force with creating something that lasts?

- Money is only part of your life's equation.

- Chasing more money will inevitably leave you making bad decisions, coming up short, and living a discontented life.

- Define what is enough for you and your family—house, cars, retirement accounts, charity, all of it. Get clear about this stuff now, so that you'll know when to stop. Involve your spouse and children in the discussions—no matter how old they are.

- At the end of your life, you likely won't be wishing you had made more money. Play your life backward from that day to today and live to avoid that kind of regret.

CHAPTER 9

Playing with Fire

"Sex is dirty, save it for someone you love!"
—UNKNOWN

Physical touch is only one of several ways we give and receive love. I am the youngest of eight kids. Since my mom was fiercely religious, she might have thought we all believed that each of her kids had been Immaculately Conceived. We weren't.

Before middle school, I was mostly oblivious to the opposite sex. I was focused on sports, school, and playing outside. Sex was talked about in my house only in hushed tones. I can't easily recall it being portrayed in a positive light. I vaguely remember hearing that women give sex to get love, and men give love to get sex. If you ask me, that represents a grim transaction on both sides of the gender ledger.

I can recall vividly my first time being alone with a girl. Sounds predictable, but it actually was with the girl next door. She invited me into her basement under the pretense of playing a game of pool. My family had a billiards table when I was younger, so the idea initially sounded great. When we got downstairs, the reality was that playing a game of eight-ball was the farthest thing from her mind.

She had strewn a half dozen lip glosses along the edge of the pool table. She eagerly informed me that she was going to put on each one, and it was my job to guess each of the flavors. To me, it sounded like a game of charades or Guess Who. Little did I know what was unfolding. I was about to be a deer in the headlights!

Fifteen minutes and six lip glosses later, I was adrift from my body. I may as well have been shot with a taser. I couldn't feel anything reliable besides my own elevated heartbeat. There was a rushing sound in my ears that left me wobbly in the knees. I was worried that my tonsils had been extracted from the back of my throat. My lips tasted as though they had been dragged across a soda fountain reservoir.

It may seem like I am making this into a big deal, but that's because for me it was. In my little mind, I went from sitting in Park to beating the street at ninety miles per hour around the hairpin turn of my impending adolescence.

My mom thought I was in the backwoods playing Cowboys and Indians. She was undoubtedly perched high above it all in the kitchen—like the Eye of Sauron in the *Lord of the Rings* series—scanning her kingdom in every direction to ensure that her kids were safe and not getting into things they shouldn't be.

How could I effectively hide from her the fact that I had just been apprehended by a thirteen-year-old Calamity Jane? There was no way I was going to pull it together enough to conceal what had just happened.

I was both frantic and exhilarated; afraid and captivated. Thankfully, my unauthorized tryst went unnoticed by the Great Eye, my mom. I eased back into the house as though nothing had happened.

I had little grasp of what had just transpired. It felt as though a meteor just cratered itself onto the surface of my childhood. The experience was a witch's brew of lost innocence, excitement, and misplaced guilt.

It would be the light-hearted harbinger of what happens when there is lust without connection. The experience marked the trailhead of my deep dive toward a troubled adolescence. Unknowingly, I had taken the next step in my journey away from myself and my private nature. It would be nearly two decades later before I put sex and my relationship with women into proper context.

When I was a kid, pornography was not as readily available as it is today. There was still a healthy sense of shame around using it; sheer embarrassment dampened the use of it as well. To see a "girly" magazine was a feat that required both a careful focus and heroic resolve. For me and my friends, it required what seemed like a six-hour bike trip, one way. Back somewhere deep in the woods, we followed a crudely sketched map to a mythic boulder. It took five of us kids to roll the rock back. Under it was a plastic bag that protected the coveted images. If you were lucky, you got sixty seconds alone with a few shirtless women you would never know.

Remembering that we had to hightail it home before dark, we would perform the ritual in reverse. Before the long, shameful ride home, my friends and I would roll the boulder back and survey the immediate area to purge any clue that we had been there. To see pornography back then, you had to be pretty sneaky.

My wife is fond of telling our kids that they can't unsee things. She is right. A few years later, access to that kind of one-sided portrayal of women amped up significantly. I wish I could have had the sense or good fortune to avoid the influences that ushered me past what I knew to be right.

Seeing barely-clothed women warped my focus for a time and reshuffled my adolescent priorities. In some ways, the unrealistic hype tangled me up and led to a diminished sense of self. I started to see the opposite sex as the axis on which my identity turned. In my then-distorted view, the women I connected with were meant to complete, validate, and heal the parts of me that were insecure and needy.

Later the next summer, an older girl in the neighborhood took advantage of me. I don't blame her; I was clearly someplace I shouldn't have been, without my wits about me. Without question, the experience shifted my need to prove myself to women into overdrive.

Exaggerating the role of sex and diminishing the intrinsic value of women is a major way some men go AWOL. Women are not objects. They are daughters, sisters, aunts, wives, mothers, and friends. They were not at fault for my brokenness, nor were they responsible for putting me back together. No matter how hard we may try, manhood is *not* bestowed onto men by women.

It's not just in the rearview mirror that objects seem larger than they actually are. The opposite sex became super exaggerated for me early in life. I handed over the power to build and crush parts of my self-worth. It was an unfair trade on both sides.

All of this was very unconscious as well. I didn't understand what was happening to me at the time. I needed valuable perspective and distance to grasp the subtext. Not until I reached my twenties was I able to reset my damaged thinking.

As I grew and matured physically, my rationalizations became even more distorted. I was somewhat one-dimensional, fixated on my body and its pleasures. Guilt turned into shame as the natural progression, and maturing turned into using and being used.

I stopped firing on important emotional and spiritual cylinders. It was as if I broke a "moral bone" and never went to the doctor to have it properly set. The deepest parts of me were greatly impacted. I wasn't the only one who would pay the price for my narrowing focus.

Clearly, as a teenager, I had taken a wrong turn in my life. I began using the opposite sex for my enjoyment. I am sad to admit that being pursued by women in high school, and then in college, made me feel cool and temporarily validated.

Their affirmations were inadequately hollow, always short-lived; the hole inside of me was far too gaping to plug up with their words or affection. Nothing from the outside could establish traction inside my dead bones. My aim had been reduced to doing and having.

Playing with Fire

I was play-acting at manhood, and despite false adulations, I had morphed into a very shallow person. I was a trainwreck and nearly everyone knew it but me. In conquering, I had been conquered.

Outwardly, I tried to act as though my self-centered existence was the real me. After all, only I knew I was a dead man walking. Sadly, the Poser was leaving an enormous wake behind him. One day, the waves would grow and rebound back toward me, capsizing my own flimsy dingy. I was saying far more with my body than I was able to convey emotionally.

It was like most things that deny our higher selves; I finally wanted off the roller coaster. I was tired of hurting others and tired of hurting myself. I was stuck on the wrong trapeze, desperate to get off, but I was unable to visualize the one swinging toward me that would be part of my escape and rescue.

So, there I was at nineteen, swinging back and forth, hoping that the rhythm of a familiar requiem would lull me back to sleep and away from the profound realization that I had quit on the me I knew I could be.

I had already lived long enough to know that lust is like eating an entire bag of barbeque potato chips. It might taste good at first, but they provide no real nourishment. Before long, you feel sick to your stomach. Downstream, the internal after-effects of your binging leave you in such pain, you swear to yourself you'll never do it again.

The difference between lust and love is the object of affection and advance. In lust, we look to satisfy ourselves; in love, it is our beloved that matters most. In lust, we love things and use people; in love, as a result of our deeper affections, we consciously reset the priority to be the good of our beloved.

Lust was a poor remedy for what was ailing me. I had confused lust with love and had lost all credibility with myself and those around me. Hurtling toward young adulthood, I was confronted with the truth. Being wanted by women was false advertising. I thought being wanted and pursued would reconnect me to me.

It didn't; instead, it drove me further away from the real me. I was ready to ditch my "hard-guy" exterior in order to relentlessly pursue my real life.

Get Busy Living!

- Our culture has taught men to be overly focused on sex. You are more than your sexuality.

- Sex can be far too easy. Misused, it is a cheap form of intimacy.

- Respect the creative force that is represented by your sex drive. Our physical desire resides deep in our ancestral hard drives. Identify it and harness it for good!

- You can reel your sex nature in and master it. Stop letting your sex drive master you. Allow it to morph into something beautiful and long-lasting.

CHAPTER 10

Getting Good at Sex

"It is not that pornography shows too much, it's that it shows too little!"
—POPE JOHN PAUL II

Our sex natures are intricately woven into our personalities and are the source of abundant levels of creative energy. We don't readily make the connection that sex energy is so powerful, or that it helps drive most of us to accomplish and succeed.

A well-known comedian joked that if he knew grandkids were going to be so awesome, he would have had them first. My kids are still young, so I can't yet speak about my experience of being a grandfather.

What I can attest to is this: If I knew that sex within marriage was going to be so awesome, I would have had it first.

Ann Marie and I have been married twenty-four years and counting. I am fortunate to have married a woman much better than me in almost every regard, but I also appreciate that not every man feels this way about his wife. I am careful not to brag; I just happily acknowledge my extreme good fortune.

But it's still early. I estimate that my wife and I are likely just approaching halftime in our married life. I know there is still a lot time left on the clock, so I am careful not to take score too early. I work hard to keep my head in the game that I most want to win.

From the outset, my wife set the moral bar high for us. On our first official date, not ten minutes into our drive, she informed me that there was a reason why previous men she'd dated lost interest in courting her.

When they learned that she valued her purity and was committed to abstaining from sex until marriage, they seemed to lose interest. What a comment on our culture's inability to delay immediate gratification in exchange for things that last.

In some ways, I believe that my early years on the well-worn road to perdition somehow galvanized my desire to marry a woman of virtue. Moving forward from adolescence, I wanted more from my primary relationship than performing and posing. If I was going to attract positive outcomes in my love life, then I was going to have to act differently. Fortunately, I came to this realization long before I met my wife.

In my youthful search for "Mrs. Right," I had the binoculars flipped backward; the oculars were focused on the smallest part of the equation. Physical attraction trumped everything else that really mattered.

I now know that the key to having a great marriage is 10 percent finding the right person and 90 percent *being* the right person.

There are countless books and resources available on sex. Some are healthy and helpful; all are appealing to our legitimate desire to get the most out of our God-given sex nature.

With the benefit of hindsight, I now view sex much like I do nuclear power. Confined and curated correctly, it can be enormously powerful without consuming other precious natural resources. It has a unique ability to perpetuate wonderful outcomes, and it can be harnessed for the benefit of the entire community. However, safeguards are key and it's critical to monitor real-time feedback of what's going on inside the reactor.

When we don't respect it, we inevitably mishandle it. The

uncontained reaction has the potential to cause a meltdown disaster like in Chernobyl, Russia. What seems like such a good idea at the time can turn into a nightmare in a flash. It can leave everything near it scorched and lifeless. Amid the false promises and illusory expectations, our hopes are dashed; we lose the important buffers that were designed to promote a higher quality of life.

The most reliable reactor in which to split or fuse our most intimate atoms, the deepest parts of us, is marriage.

There is a well-formed delusion running rampant in our culture: The idea that marriage is meant to complete us and somehow make us whole. Moreover, we are led to believe that sex is the biggest determinant of whether or not our marriage has what it takes to go the distance. It's obvious that attraction is very important initially, but to make it the litmus test of our most important bond is much too narrow a focus.

I love the illustration of fractionated people entering marriage. In middle school math, we learned that when you multiply fractions, they get smaller. So one-half times one-half equals one-quarter. The same holds true in marriage. When half a man marries half a woman, both hoping they will become a whole number, the product is instead a smaller fraction.

Going AWOL results in us being less than a whole person. When we look to our wives to complete us, we are set up for frustration and disappointment. Our marriage won't solve our issues, it will reveal them.

I never knew math was such a big part of sex education until later in life.

Let's say that a husband and wife enjoy a very active sex life. I think any married person would agree that sex three times a week would be a generous estimate of a healthy sex life.

Let's also assume that each of their intimate encounters lasts an average of forty-five minutes—again, a generous estimate.

When you review the math embedded in this time study, this means that less than 2 percent of his life will be spent having sex with his wife.

The dominant space that sex occupies in our minds is wildly disproportionate to our actual experiences. Remember that the 2 percent reflects the upper limits of sexual activity in marriage. We had better find something more dependable to measure the success of our marriages than the time we spend having sexual intercourse.

Thanks to our culture's limitless preoccupation with casual sex and pornography, we have dumbed down the transformational, unseen power baked into the procreative and co-creative act of sexual relations. We run wildly over sexual terrain and minimize its dramatic and long-lasting impact on individuals and couples alike.

As a result, we seek new and imaginative ways to delimit our seemingly unrestrainable sex natures. We may ask our wives to contracept, or husbands to use a condom to free us to have sex whenever we want, never considering that this ushers in a whole new level of physical and emotional complexities. Most resentments of this type are unconscious and seldom bubble to the surface to be expressed or discussed until it's too late.

Many men go to the urologist for a vasectomy thinking that they are being given a "golden ticket" to renewed sexual freedom—forgetting that things that seem too good to be true usually are. Some honest couples I have met are emphatic when tracing their ailing marriages and sex lives to the time when they surgically neutralized the husband's sex nature and potency.

I can't judge; only you know if you are acting for the good of your partner or out of your own self-interest, but it's worth your serious consideration.

I know that when we are unconscious of the impact, we become poor stewards of the gift we have been given in our sex natures. We disrespect ourselves and our spouses when we relegate sex to just another form of exercise, personal wellness, or entertainment. It's a shame that men are so adept at recognizing and respecting cause and effect in almost every other area of their lives besides their own bedrooms.

Promiscuity before and during marriage wreaks havoc in multiple ways.

Today, many non-denominational churches report record numbers of married men who are seeking help because they can't perform in the bedroom due to the damaging effect of pornography on their sex-drives. Many young men have lost their desire to discover their vocation and purpose, choosing to hole up in their parents' basements to play video games instead.

Record numbers of marriages dissolve when couples lose sexual attraction to each other. There is a big connection between our bids for attention and the physical connections we make with our spouse. Part of what makes a spark exciting is the potential for all-out ignition.

I wonder if stunting the procreative potency of sex and the mystery that the act embodies has stunted the entire creative process for both men and women. Again, are we consuming or are we being consumed? There is no way to use without also being used.

But there is hope. Between 1930 and 1950, it seemed as though the entire world smoked cigarettes. They were marketed as good for men and women; hard to believe, but doctors' recommendations about the health benefits were often paired with the world's deadliest consumer product. Can you imagine that the benefits of smoking were, in recent history, viewed by doctors as legitimate?

As a kid, it seemed like everyone smoked. My dad smoked on the edge of his bed at the beginning and end of his day. My high school-aged siblings smoked openly in front of my parents. Professional athletes smoked during competitions. I can recall smoking sections on an airplane, in restaurants, and in offices.

Today, you can barely smoke in public.

How did consumer sentiment and the medical establishment turn against this massive industry seemingly overnight? I'm not a pathologist, but evidently, the correlation was made between smoking and terminal diseases such as lung cancer. The medical community owned up to what amounted to bad medicine; they could no longer evade the truth. People realized there was something unhealthy and damaging that was previously billed as "good for us."

Same with sex. Could we be in a phase similar to cigarette smoking in the early seventies? Maybe we should start considering what's at stake in regard to casual sex. What is good for us is often not popular, and what is popular rarely leads to what is best for us.

How long will we refuse to admit the damage we do to ourselves and others by not respecting our sex natures?

Please don't discount what I am saying—I am not against sex. I am a big fan. My wife and I have been pregnant twelve times and have seven beautiful children. We're not Amish. Sex isn't verboten. We really enjoy being together.

I'm not a fun extinguisher, either.

I am merely trying to shine a light on the overgrown, seldom-used path that leads to the real treasure in marriage. As men, we don't have to remain captive to the role that sex occupies in our thought lives. We can grab ahold of the reins of our runaway horses. We can return to the place where we have a more solid grasp on our sex impulses. We can again, or for the first time, steward our "nuclear energy" for good.

Our wives want to be pursued. How will there ever be fireworks between us if we fail to keep our sex energy focused and in check? To paraphrase Pope John Paul II at the top of this chapter: When we disrespect our sex natures, it's not that we go too far, it's that we don't go far enough. It's not that we see too much, it's that we see far too little.

Get Busy Living!

- Resist the world's fixation with turning sex into solely a physical act. It is a bodily manifestation of something much deeper.

- Recognize that intimacy is really a profound way to express and receive love.

- Do you ever talk with your wife about your hopes for your sex life? Do you ever let her express hers?

- Don't degrade the deepest parts of you. Allow room in your life for the good stuff that outlasts mere physical beauty and sexual attraction.

- Recognize the transactions you are making without the consent of your soul. Your body is not your master. Do not let it control you or diminish your experience of intimacy.

CHAPTER 11

Weighing Your Insides

"All of man's problems stem from his inability to sit alone in a dark room in silence."

—BLAISE PASCAL

The topics of religion and spirituality are the hardest for me to write about. The rub for me is that it is deeply personal and hard to describe without coming across as preachy. Plus, there are already so many great books written on the topic that it seems nearly impossible to chart new territory or add additional depth. I believe it's risky to try to get men past more than a faint acknowledgment of their spiritual natures.

Having been previously disconnected spiritually, I know that this aspect of our existence can be easy to punt. It is hard to agree on events that defy explanation or truths that emanate from another dimension. It is also important to acknowledge that the rigor of spiritual disciplines can feel outdated and sometimes opposed to our quest for material success or something we are trying to accomplish on our outsides.

Many men I know characterize their lives as being mostly on the physical and mental planes. Granted, they would acknowledge a few emotional and spiritual experiences sprinkled in along the way, but the occasional spiritual moments are like random bottle rockets, appearing momentarily before falling lifeless to the ground.

Spiritual truths do exist; but if we are not ready to consider them, they can repel us rather than attract us.

The reality is that we have a natural resistance to go deep, because the soul gains we make are likely to be known only to us. There are no external scoreboards for time spent alone listening to and cultivating a relationship with God. Winning spiritually is an inside game, and those kinds of contests aren't very attractive to men, at least initially.

As I have grown spiritually, I've found two clear states of being: I am either plugged into my Source or I am unplugged. I am either running my show, or I am taking my cues from The Showman.

I readily admit that I have long resisted being alone. I rarely liked the time I spent with just myself, at home or in church. It was hard for me to experience calm when I retreated into the stillness of my own company. My first defense was to claim that my lack of peace was due to a natural preference for activity and getting things done. I have a high motor and would, by nature, rather "do" than "be."

I could make a similar argument for staying away from the gym. I don't naturally want to wake up early, pack an extra bag, jump in a cold pool, swim for an hour, and shower before starting my workday. Being physically healthy takes intention, preparation, and effort.

But things are easier in the gym. There is a circuit we follow. Without much thought, we fall into a routine that suits us and delivers visible results. We hit it hard and, before long, we either see or feel outward progress.

In the right measure, this is all very healthy and life-giving. Looking fit on the outside and doing challenging things gives each of us a desired daily singular dose of accomplishment. Real-time feedback, so black-and-white, is hard to come by. We get to check a box, and it feels great.

As men, we love things that have a clear beginning, middle, and end.

For me, an added motivation is that when I don't show up to swim, I get razzed the next day by one of the other pool regulars. Thus, I'm doubly upset with myself if I fail to get to the pool.

In comparison, there is little about the spiritual life that delivers such tangible rewards. The spiritual pace is often times glacial, and evidence of the cause and effect that comes from spending time in solitude can easily evade us. Sadly, many men discount their faith well before they develop enough spiritual muscle.

Everything that encourages us to take action with our bodies is turned upside down in soul work.

There is little correlation that others make between my spiritual life and the way I present to the world around me. It's not like my spiritual muscles show up physically like my biceps do. The failure to take my spiritual nature seriously appears inside me as invisible symptoms or a nagging sense that my life lacks depth and meaning.

When I miss a day of prayer and meditation, I think nobody notices. Truthfully though, the first couple of days, I notice. A few days later, my wife and kids notice. Give me a week without connecting on deep levels inside, and almost everyone notices. I can quickly lose my spiritual footing and bearings, and it shows up as me being short-tempered, anxious, and pushy.

For those who have not spent time or energy nurturing their soul lives, getting started can feel daunting and scary. At times, thinking about our mortalities and our places in eternity feels overwhelming and impossible to wrap our arms around.

I often recall my close friend, Father Jim's, sage advice and stern warning as Ann Marie and I prepared for marriage.

We were just a few months away from getting married. He

told us a short story that has proven to be extremely valuable. He painted a picture of my life being like a football game where I was the quarterback. He told me that evil wasn't interested in the spectators at a football game; it wasn't even interested in the coaches or other players. Evil was focused solely on the quarterback. Sacking the quarterback isn't enough, either. Evil wants to take the quarterback out of the game!

I don't want to be out of the game, I want to play.

Take that football analogy a bit further and consider that the helmets of NFL quarterbacks are wired with one-way radios. Coaches in the press box, high above the game are able to instruct and encourage their quarterbacks between plays. From a higher vantage point, they provide real-time feedback, plan strategy, inform their on-field "gunslinger" of what they see developing on the field.

This is how I view prayer and meditation. The time I spend in solitude is where I keep my spiritual antenna tuned in to the higher frequency. Inroads on the spiritual front are hard-fought and do not come easily. The only way to develop this relationship is by spending time. We have lost the notion that making room for spirituality and religion is really about building a relationship.

If I am going to grow spiritually,
I must get comfortable with being uncomfortable.

If I want to grow along spiritual lines, I need to put in the time. I must make room for my spiritual development. I need to spend more time unplugged from busyness and plugged into the Source.

I retreat most days to a special place at our home that fosters this connection. I read each day from a devotional that makes my relationship with God more personal and interactive. It helps me cut through all the other noise and chatter that distracts me.

By doing this, I learn so much about God's nature.

I know I need to spend time with God. I don't always need to understand what is going on in my life either, because I can trust God. I needn't complicate things, and I don't need to look too far ahead. I should be grateful regardless of what is going on around me, for there is always something about which to be grateful.

Moments of anxiousness provide me with opportunities to grow and trust. I remind myself that I am not in control, but I can choose to rejoice in the midst of hardships. I can breathe deeply and think calm thoughts regardless of my circumstances. Life, despite my emotions, is unfolding as it should. It's okay to feel empty. God's abundance and my emptiness are well suited for one another. I can be candid with God. He can take it! It's okay if I slow down and enjoy the journey. In fact, it's God's plan for my life. I am being led along a path that is prepared uniquely for me.

There is a funny story I have told many times of a young boy in church. He is only five years old and is sandwiched into a small pew up front with his mother and father. Halfway through one Sunday service, the boy gets bored with the sermon. His mom seems to have lost her usual focus on him, so he stands up and turns to face the rest of his fellow churchgoers.

He begins making funny faces; in a matter of seconds, his antics have captured the attention of almost the entire congregation. The muffled laughter from behind his pew finally gets his mother's attention. In a flash, she grabs him by the arm and swats him across his bottom. He wails and cries. Evidently satisfied with the result of her chastisement, his mother turns to him and hisses over his wailing, "That's more like it!"

Rules without relationship equals rebellion.

If men feel like that little boy—believing that church is just rules, regulations, duties, and punishments—is it any wonder they have admitted to "checking out" when asked if they go to church regularly on Sundays?

I have spent a ton of time in church. I have always been drawn there, as I sense an indescribable presence alive there. In church, I somehow suspend the disbelief of my senses and consider timeless truths; they rouse and transform me.

But for many men who run aground, it's counterintuitive to turn inward. It's more logical to ramp up efforts in the material world. Prayer and meditation are often the last resort.

In tough times, we hear, "I guess there is nothing left to do but pray!" As if someone has to be really desperate to pray. I would argue that the time to develop a relationship with your best friend is before you need Him!

For me, the gateway to my spiritual life is to actively still my body. It has become a profound part of my daily discipline. My body is forever clamoring for my attention. Left in charge, it demands constant recognition. When I unplug its microphone, the Spirit gently instructs the body that it is not leading me, that there exists a deeper and eternal part inside me that has a greater wisdom and authority.

If I am not doing anything, God is—and that's the entire point.

Let me be clear, sitting alone in a dark room in a wakeful state can still be unnerving. Though it's no less of a challenge than working out at the gym at 5:00 a.m. or swimming a mile in a cold pool. Befriending silence, stillness, and solitude leads to the rich inner life that awaits us on the other side of resisting it.

From time to time, I try to picture my soul stepping on a scale. How heavy am I? I want to be spiritually dense; I want my soul to gain some eternal mass.

My soul is where my internal fire burns. We describe certain things as being "soulless," or we recount jobs that have "robbed us of our souls," or people who have "crushed our souls." What a "soul" is, exactly, remains elusive, and therein lies its attraction and beauty.

If we could define it, we'd be limited by some humdrum notion of what soul and God mean. What matters is that they exist and that we seek to know both.

Weighing Your Insides

I have found nothing crowds my soul's development out faster than STUFF and the energy it takes to acquire and maintain the material things that vie for my attention and resources.

Here's a gut check. How many minutes do you spend each week nourishing and tending to the parts deep inside of you? Where do you do this? Perhaps you think there is something to be scared of inside or that acknowledging these more meaningful parts is a sign of weakness.

This flawed notion keeps us from tapping into the most loving and unconditional force in the universe. We forget that our souls were intended to be the safest places for us to land. It makes me sad to think that so many men have been denied access to the deepest parts of their being. Our soul lives should stand separate and distinct from our active lives.

Personally, what often drives me out of the spiritual realm is fear that my efforts are in vain or that I am relinquishing control. I battle with this and likely will until my last breath. But attention paid to the spiritual realm is exponential and accretive. It both makes no sense and the most sense, simultaneously.

If you are spiritually AWOL, here's a way to get back on track:

Honor and make room for your spiritual development. Carve out time for silence and solitude. Be intentional. Start small and let your internal fire build over time.

Kneeling humbles us; it helps us to remember where our gifts come from.

The younger version of me was inordinately focused on trying to convert folks to my way of thinking and believing. Now I know it is not my job to convert anyone.

These days, I mostly just want my life to speak. I don't need to beat anyone up with my faith. Part of me resisting ever again going AWOL spiritually is staying in my own lane and trusting that a power far greater than me is at work in the world.

I try to keep an active internal dialogue going with God throughout my day. I am watching, waiting, and asking for directions. I'm resolved to stay in conscious contact with His Infinite Intelligence. Thankfully, if I persist and remain open and accessible, communication becomes a two-way street.

Get Busy Living!

- Make room in your life to unplug from the noise and plug back into the "still, small voice" inside you.

- Persisting in prayer and meditation changes your world; inside and out.

- Decide to make time and space to quiet your body in contemplative prayer.

- God speaks to us in silence and solitude; identify a spot to do this work.

- Do you have a set time of day to meet with God on a regular basis?

- What are you most afraid God might ask you to do?

- Jesus isn't lost, we are. Call out to him and trust that getting you home safely is no longer just your problem.

CHAPTER 12

Other Dead-End Roads

"Successful people do that which unsuccessful people are unwilling to do!"
—JOHN MAXWELL

There are innumerable ways we can distract ourselves from our most important work. Hobbies and interests can imperceptibly cross an imaginary line that turns good things into bad habits that can eventually damage and control us.

On the brink of a deep dive into what's involved in our intentional return from being AWOL, I think it's important to take a quick look at some other ways some men check out on themselves and their families.

I recognize that playing and relaxing are important. Setting heavy things down for a while helps us pick them back up again, more intelligently.

Sometimes forgetting is a great way to remember.

What follows is *not* meant to be an old-man rant. My intent is not to alienate or condemn. Only you know if any of these behaviors have veered you off course from the journey you are meant to take.

Read the following list and its descriptions. Try each on. If they don't fit, dismiss them.

If one or two hit closer to home, linger on them, and determine if they have pushed you out of balance. Bad habits start small; they don't even show up on the radar at first. That's the best time to pluck them out of your life, before they capture you and prevent you from showing up for yourself in more meaningful ways.

Alcohol: I have many friends who are pastors and priests. The really good ones are concerned about the prominence of alcohol in the lives of men. Since when did bourbon become a religion?

I have noted over the past three or four Halloweens that some fathers have developed an inability to get around the neighborhood for Trick or Treating without pulling a wagon behind them. It's not their kids that are in the wagon. It's their cooler.

It's important for us to unwind, and alcohol can be effective in helping us peel off our game face and get out of grind mode. Most of the stupid things I did as a young man were alcohol-induced, so admittedly I am a bit jaded. Still, the incredible lack of judgment while being buzzed or under the influence doesn't disappear as we get older. In fact, there is much more to lose from poor judgment.

Our kids are watching, along with everyone on our social media feeds. Alcohol is a common way men can avoid the feelings of being depleted and numb. It can be used to mask the deep regret of who we have become. It's odd that as a society, we consume massive amounts of different variations of this depressant and wonder why everyone around us is so depressed.

Sports: Sports are a great way to develop physically. Moreover, they provide us with incredible backdrops on which we project our character. We learn so much about ourselves and others by competing in athletics.

I really enjoy watching football and other sports, but I try hard to keep it in the proper perspective. It seems increasingly clear that sports have become the gods of the present age. It used to be that churches dominated the skylines of our major cities; now, they have all been dwarfed by multi-billion-dollar sports arenas.

People are fanatics about their teams. Maybe we have crossed a line of the importance we should place on our sports and the athletes who play them. The jerseys, the indelible face paint, the $250 game ticket, and the $10,000 trip for two to the Super Bowl might invite us to wonder if we have lost our perspective on the importance of a game.

Glory days (high school or college): Done right, school provides us with wonderful opportunities to learn and grow. But we become prone to glorify the past when our future dries up.

Some men live for the annual weekend pilgrimage back to campus for the big home game. Like the lyrics of a Bruce Springsteen song, maybe they long for the glory days when they felt more connected to the idea of a bright future where success would come easy to them.

The recent phenomenon of perpetual adolescence (college, part 2): There is no doubt that a fraternity with a great group of guys is important and life-giving. My friends are hugely important to me, and I love the time I get to spend with them. But at what point do we turn in our card-carrying membership to adolescence?

What signals to us that we are officially men? Perpetual adolescence shows up in more ways than bringing a cooler of beer to prayer meetings or to our kids' high school football games. If you want to be a good husband and father, then overscheduling weekend-long golf outings or jaunts to Wrigley Field can lead to you focus on the wrong things.

I know a once successful dentist who lost his marriage and dental practice because he would not come out of his basement. He spent nearly two years playing *Call of Duty* with his college buddies. His life became a raging dumpster fire.

I see some of the same guys in the gym at different times of the day. They admit to being in the gym two or sometimes three times a day. It makes me wonder who is paying the price for our chiseled biceps or our three handicaps in golf.

Technology: Men naturally gravitate toward having the

latest gadgets. We are enchanted by the idea that we can get the important quadrants of our lives to sync more effectively. It also plays nicely with our natural tendencies toward attention deficit disorder.

We have invested heavily in time-saving devices and apps, yet are any of us sitting on a reserve of unspent time as a result of the investment?

I was floored to discover that most high-level executives at the ten biggest tech companies won't allow their children to have devices or access to social media until they are well into their teens. They must be privy to the negative long-term effects of these addictive platforms.

At some point, it's important to step back and analyze the complexity of our lives and decide if we are going to use technology or let technology use us and our families. Maybe the time has come for us to combat what's hijacked us.

Television: Back in high school, I remember a boy relating a story about his enraged father from the night before. He said that he and his family had been huddled up before dinner watching some sitcom when his dad came home from a long day at the office. Upon entering the family room, he said hello to his family but received no response. Some grumbling ensued, and they all mindlessly assumed it was their dad out in the garage making the tremendous racket.

Just then, Dad reappeared wearing a large pair of leather work gloves and hedge shears. He worked his way behind the screen and severed the power cord. Amid a cloud of sparks and smoke, his dad ripped the TV off the wall mount and proceeded to launch it through the front door where it smashed in the yard. He looked at his family, all with mouths gaping wide open, and said, "Tomorrow night when I get home, I bet you'll say hello to me."

TVs have become the center of our homes. What are we thinking, building our family rooms around technology that has the potential to divide and distance us from one another so radically?

Living through our kids: Watching our kids excel in sports or other extracurriculars is thrilling. Seeing them pursue the things they are passionate about is life-giving. But all of the excitement can get out of hand in a hurry.

Have you been to a third-grade football game recently? Have you seen how parents and coaches have lost their perspective on the important way sports shape and develop our children's characters and sense of team?

I have seen a guy's veins protruding a full inch from his neck over some boy dropping an errant pass. I have watched dads in the stands openly "coach" their sons in opposition to the play their coach just called—then watched the kid's eyes dart back and forth from coach to dad, afraid to upset either man. The drama can border on insanity. Winning at all costs is subtly inbred; in so doing, we lose the opportunity to teach our kids that character is forged in how we win and lose.

Gambling: An old friend of mine was consumed by gambling. He fell behind quickly but was determined to get his money back. It was just a matter of time, he thought. At $20,000 down, he had burned through all of his short-term savings. Then he dipped into his home's equity line and lost another $80,000. When I lost touch with him, he had borrowed an additional $220,000 from his 401(k) to cover his gambling addiction. He was unable to admit that he was cornered and locked into a lose/lose game. His habit had been no big deal until it was too strong for him to break.

Cars and material things: Cars are super cool and driving a mean machine is a whole lot of fun. Quickly, though, our stuff can start feeling like an extension of who we are. But it isn't, it's just stuff.

Popular brands capitalize on this and feed our need to project the right image. We pay handsomely to be seen driving the right car, wearing the right clothes, or belonging to the right golf club. Soon, we think that by covering our outsides with what others perceive as luxury and privilege, we can make up for the inadequacy we feel inside.

Trying to gather enough of the right stuff has the potential to make us crazy and broke. The rat race leaves us speeding in our leased Porsche down a dead-end street—all to impress folks who we didn't even like that much in the first place.

Hunting and fishing: Some friends and relatives of mine are legit hunters; the intent is to commune with nature and economically fill the family freezer with high-quality, lean protein. Other guys I know are overly geeked out on all the stuff they get to buy in support of their favorite pastimes. They own several coats, pairs of boots, guns, bows, ozone-makers, scopes, stands, rods, reels, boats, and other expensive gear.

Like the bucks they are hunting, these men stumble through Cabela's as if they are in rut themselves—only it isn't a doe they are chasing, it's more gear!

People-pleasing and martyrdom: This one can be really hard to pin down because it is cloaked in what appears to be life-giving and admirable. There is a big difference between being a martyr and a victim. There is very little virtue in letting others run over us. Willfully giving our lives in service to others is incredibly valuable and noble. But, believing that we can earn our way into our own good grace by checking out in the service of others is counterproductive and eventually leaves us feeling used and dissatisfied.

I am certain that this list is still incomplete. The ways we can check out on ourselves are as innumerable as the turning points that sent us AWOL in the first place. What matters is that we recognize that going AWOL and staying AWOL are related. Each is rooted in the belief that we are flawed and lacking, and this deficiency can be made up by something outside of us. It's those two beliefs that lead to our malaise and dysfunction.

Get Busy Living!

- It can be hard to determine when we have crossed the line between enjoying our passions and hobbies and letting them spiral out of control.

- We are meant to have fun. We are designed to be in pursuit of good things and to feel fully alive. Do you feel like you're in balance in this respect?

- If you are married, what does your wife think? Your kids? Will you ask them? If they can be candid, then their feedback will be invaluable.

- Stay in communication with other men who you view as trusted voices. Give them permission to speak their truth to you.

young life, I found a way to work for men who were unable to help me solve the discontent inside of me. How could they? It was never their job. I paid an excessive price to grasp this enduring truth:

Work is a terrible place to get your emotional needs met.

I must have a freakishly high pain tolerance because I withstood many years playing out my roles in this recurring narrative. Not until much later in life was I able to connect the dots between my going AWOL as a kid and how it manifested again and again in my adult career choices. I never would have admitted to being complicit in the drama that left me feeling disrespected, depleted, and unappreciated at work.

My good buddy, Randy, is a very successful businessman. He loves to tell a story of how he fought the same battle early in his career. He started his entrepreneurial effort with some quick success but had trouble scaling his business. Not knowing what to do, he hired a business consultant. Forty-five minutes into the engagement, the consultant arrived in his office and said she had already uncovered his limiting factor: "It's you!"

He fired her on the spot. Two years passed, and his company continued to rise and fall. Oddly, he reached back out to the original consultant to have another whack at identifying his company's enduring dysfunction. Purposefully, without recalling too much of her original assignment, she jumped in with both feet. In less than two hours she returned to my friend with a oddly familiar verdict: "You're the problem, and everyone knows it!"

He fired her again and doubled down on his limited view of how the business should operate.

Fifteen months later, with his tail between his legs, he could no longer postpone or evade the truth. His eyes were open. He was the problem. It was his own narrative and self-perception that were reenacting the broken parts inside him on the outside and in the lives of those around him.

In my earlier years, my hurt felt so big that I avoided ever making eye contact with it. My past pain had me convinced that if I tried to get my arms around it, I might be totally overwhelmed. What a load of BS! I didn't realize I had endured the worst of it already. Whatever it had to teach me was coming from a good place, the part that wanted my real self to emerge.

The pain wants out and it will do all it can to get us to turn around and ask, "What do you want to teach me?"

My pressing goal was to retrieve valuable artifacts from my early battlefields I had ignored for far too long.

The courageous parts of me yearned to go back to ground zero. The fear was amping up the volume that called me back home. I am not sure why pain is set up to play such a pivotal role in getting us back to sea level inside ourselves, but it does.

It's unclear to me if pain forces itself upon us as an uninvited guest or if it turns up on our internal doorsteps in response to a deeper, unconscious invitation from some part inside of us. My experience has shown me that the truth wants nothing more than to have our insides and outsides match.

In the classic English poem, *Beowulf*, the mythical warrior is hired by Hrothgar, the King of Denmark, to restore peace to his kingdom. A terrible beast named Grendel has been tormenting the king and his subjects night after night. The grotesque and powerful creature lives in a lifeless swamp and swoops in each night to have his way with the men, women, and children.

Beowulf and his men carefully prepare for Grendel's impending return. They set up their ambush in the great hall of King Hrothgar's palace. That first night, Beowulf mortally wounds the great beast and sends Grendel limping back to its death in a far-off swamp.

Rejoicing cascades out of the palace and across the entire kingdom and beyond. But for Beowulf, like many of us, the celebration is premature.

The Pain That Comes for You

He has failed to realize that Grendel had a mother, and she's twice as ferocious. The epic tale goes on to describe the heroic efforts of Beowulf as he confronts and slays the beast's progenitor. In the end, he succeeds, although his trusted sword melts in his hands as he chases her underwater.

The epic poem isn't only about the things we fear. It is also about the mother of our fears—the thing that birthed them.

Finding and confronting the mother of the beast— the false narrative that originally sent us running from ourselves—is the real hero's challenge.

Like Beowulf, I celebrated too early in my own life. On the surface, I had successfully conquered the parts of me that embarrassed me most. I went all in on a new version of me that projected an image of having things together to the outside world.

I got serious about my faith. I poured my best energy into my work. I fell in love and married an incredible woman. We grew and nurtured a beautiful family, and we invested in people and drew an expansive circle of love around us.

But despite all this, I could not outrun a sneaking suspicion that I was still a fraud. I felt as though I was playing one of those giant games of Jenga, except this one was on a large turntable that shook to increase exponentially the degree of difficulty. Getting real was so hard. Unconsciously, I bobbed and weaved to outmaneuver anything that thwarted a projection of my outward success.

Suffering from a condition known only to me, I was resolved to outlast the barrage of accusations that came from within me. My internal dialogue was relentless and riddled with harsh judgment, self-criticism, and doubt. I couldn't easily muster the courage to validate myself.

Many days, I wasn't sure how much longer I could keep myself together. I prayed for a spiritual "MacGyver" to rescue me and orchestrate my great escape from the pain locker I had fabricated

Get Busy Living!

- It doesn't matter how long you have been carrying this burden, the worst is over.

- Trust that fear and pain are colluding to bring about what you secretly desire most.

- Where does it hurt? How long has it hurt? Who hurt you?

- Write it down, name it, and own it. To break its grip on you, you have to give it a voice.

- It is okay to be nervous or afraid, to not know what the future holds.

- No success on your outsides will make up for failure on your insides.

- It is time to get real about what really matters.

CHAPTER 14

The Poser Taps Out!

> "You do what you can for as long as you can, and when you finally can't, you do the next best thing. You back up – but you don't give up."
> —CHUCK YEAGER

There are times when we need the emotional or spiritual equivalent of the Heimlich Maneuver. Instead, men who already find it hard to breathe put themselves into a choke hold, hoping their buried and authentic parts will give up the fight to become fully integrated into their lives.

We think that by abandoning what we perceive as the "weak parts" of ourselves, they will go away and stop working so hard to get our attention. They won't. Unless we address them and invite them into our consciousness, we will be doomed to play an exhausting game of emotional and spiritual whack-a-mole.

My kids are big fans of the various superhero movies—those supercharged productions that bring Spider-Man, Iron Man, Thor, and other great comic book characters from the Saturday mornings of our childhood to life. I have grown to enjoy them; they have been fun to watch with my kids, and I appreciate some of the deeper themes.

Personally, I am a fan of Iron Man and the role he has in the lives of his fellow superheroes. Iron Man is also businessman

Tony Stark. He's a good mix of both fun and virtue. He stands for things that last and provides a good example for his team.

In addition to being pretty cool, he is also instrumental in the life of Peter Parker, the teenager who, unbeknownst to everyone else, is Spider-Man. Imagine how cool it would be to be fifteen years old and have the incredibly powerful attributes of Spider-Man at your fingertips. I bet I wouldn't have lasted five minutes before I did something stupid or self-aggrandizing.

At one point, Peter Parker mistakenly misuses his power and privilege without discretion. After his misstep, he is confronted by his not-too-happy boss, Iron Man. In the scene, Tony Stark steps out of his Iron Man body armor and calmly breaks the bad news to Peter: "I need the [Spider-Man] suit back, Peter." Peter pleads with him, "This is all I have; I am nothing without the suit!" Stark shoots back, "If you are nothing without the suit, then you shouldn't have had it in the first place."

I have wrestled with similar conflicts many times. I had convinced myself to hold on to a successful appearance despite knowing it was no longer in my long-term best interest.

I tricked myself into believing that my value came from the image I projected. I imagined that giving up my facade would be disastrous. After all, nobody but me could prove I was counterfeiting my existence.

Despite building my identity on highly apparent and culturally acceptable strongholds, I still felt utterly vulnerable. I was unaware of how I had hemmed myself in by acquiescing to such damaging and poorly-formed beliefs about who I actually was.

I was like an addict who never really felt the depth of his own desperation. Sadly, others didn't see it either. Early on, I was honestly unaware that I was totally addicted to the fleeting intoxication I got from winning positive feedback from others. The little boy in me was still starving for a positive set point.

How easy it can be for us to overly identify with what we do—or even worse, with what others perceive us to be. The longer we stay in character, the harder it is for us to believe there is a way

The Poser Taps Out!

out of the small bit part we are playing in our own lives. For me, though, it is far different from what is portrayed in comic-based movies.

The image of the impervious superhero that I projected put access to my superpowers mostly out of reach. The further I got from the authentic me, the weaker I became.

Living and breathing inside my cheap disguise was my Kryptonite. I was in the strangest fight ever. I was battling myself, and we were both getting our butts kicked!

While I risk sounding like a comic book aficionado, around age forty-five, I started to wonder what would happen when the people around me saw that I was *not* Superman. Would they love and accept me even when I showed up only as the mild-mannered Clark Kent? What would they think if I was just a regular guy who had lost something really important and valuable? How would they respond when they realized I was determined to recover my true, authentic self?

Interesting, isn't it, that Superman is perpetually in a hurry? He is constantly vacillating between the meek version of himself and his bigger-than-life alter ego, Superman.

He is either less than or more than. He never feels like it's possible to loosen up, to be comfortable in his own skin—to just be!

Many recovering alcoholics admit to cycling through the highs and lows of feeling like egomaniacs with inferiority complexes. A well-known psychologist refers to individuals posturing between two opposing poles in their primary relationships as being "one-up or one-down." Alternating between passive and aggressive behaviors is a common default in the workplace and in other social settings. If we remain curious, then these drastic swings in our life experience can point us toward what may be suffocating us.

As we sort things out, it is important that we not view backing up in our lives as giving up. I believe that honestly and bravely revisiting the early experiences that have defined and limited us is a supreme act of courage. This mental and emotional work is no joke; to stare down your past isn't wimpy or soft. On the contrary, it may be the bravest and toughest work you will ever do as a man.

Getting more of what has not worked won't work.

When did we start to think we could bully our inner coward into becoming strong? Tapping out of a fight that I can't win isn't cowardice; in my view, it's heroic!

When I finally conceded to myself and confided in those closest to me that I was getting worn down, things started getting very real. I was halfway through the journey of my life, and I wanted more from the time I had left.

I was exhibiting signs of submission. The thought of becoming authentic had me feeling both fiercely exhilarated and scared out of my mind. Despite sensing that there was no way out, I could see subtle cracks in the veneer of what had me trapped. The healing light was breaking in, and I loved it.

A shift occurs almost immediately once we admit to being sick and tired of being sick and tired. Many men I meet are choking on the comparison of their insides with someone else's outsides. If you are still reading, then you know I struggled with this for a long time too.

What works against us as men is the popular credo that winners never quit, and quitters never win. But the virtue of never giving up must sometimes yield to the parts inside of us that know when we need to tap out and give up the fight.

From time to time, at the gym or in restaurants, I see UFC fights televised. I mean it when I say that those guys seem to be from another planet. I wonder if they ever get to be vulnerable; they seem to be Navy SEALs on a steady drip of human growth hormones.

What is it like for these guys each time they tap out and admit they have been whipped? How does it feel to watch and rewatch yourself getting pummeled by an overwhelming force? To admit you can't take the fight for one more second must involve a potent

The Poser Taps Out!

mixture of disappointment and shame, especially when viewed in prime time.

I have felt this same pummeling mentally and emotionally. The beatings were private; they were my own verbal thrashings. Thankfully, they were not televised. But as I tried to make eye contact with my own internal referee to signal that I was tapping out, the imaginary referee looked at me and shrugged, as if to say, "What do you want me to do? You're the only one who can actually stop the fight."

The weird thing is, tapping out doesn't end our fight; instead, it signals the start of the main event.

I have found that this was the most challenging part of the return to the authentic version of me. When I was at the end of my rope, all my half-measures to outrun the shame and posing stopped working—I was out of gas. I was reluctant to pick myself up and enter the ring again, especially knowing what was at stake.

I know several people in Alcoholics Anonymous. These good folks had been pinned flat on their backs by their addictions. They found that despite wanting to, they could not stop drinking. Finally, they could no longer postpone or evade the truth.

Addicts rarely recover until they bottom out. The world around them crashes, and it becomes apparent that they must either change or die. They have no idea what the new versions of themselves might look like, because at that point their lives feel like raging dumpster fires. The fortunate ones come to their senses, despite not knowing what lies ahead or who they will discover on the other side of recovery.

Some of the most amazing comeback stories I have heard come from friends and family in addiction recovery.

Our allegiance to posing presents a resistance so strong that we can negotiate on its behalf, even in the face of our death. There is a great story that helps illustrate what it feels like when we exhaust our inventory of personal resources.

A man falls off a tall cliff and is gaining speed as he plummets into the jagged rock valley below. Instinctively, he reaches out to try to grab something to save him. Miraculously, he catches his grip on a sturdy root jutting out of the sheer rock face. In disbelief, he hangs there for a few moments trying to get his mind around the fortuitous turn of events that just saved him.

Without thinking, he looks up and calls out to the cloudless blue sky above him, "God, I am not much of a believer, but if you are up there and can hear me, I sure would appreciate it if you could give me a little guidance on what to do here." A few moments pass, and then he hears, "Yes my son, I am here!" The man knows down deep that the voice he hears must be the voice of God.

Humbled and grateful, he asks the Almighty what he should do next. At this point, he is straining to keep his grip. The next ten seconds crawl by as if it were an eternity. The powerful and reassuring voice finally responds, "My son, let go of the root!"

Ten more seconds pass and the man returns his gaze to the sky above and yells, "Is there anybody else up there?"

On the edge of surrendering, we start negotiating. We start listening to the scared parts of us that want to believe that there must be an easier and softer way. Surely, we can find a less painful way back or forward.

We need to leverage the opportunities we've been given to reset the trajectory of our lives.

The hardest thing about having gone AWOL is the belief system that comes with it. I falsely believed that my rocket fuel came from the fear that something was going to overtake me. I thought that if I took away the Poser, my desire and ability to succeed would wither away to nothing.

Many men at the top of their games suffer immensely as they try to stay there. Fried on the insides, some are playing "not to lose" and feel disoriented from the internal pressure generated by posing.

The Poser Taps Out!

Tapping out is risky. The devil we know often seems better than the devil we don't. As counterintuitive as it seemed, I let go of the root I was holding on to. More accurately, it was ripped from my hands, and I was on my way down. I tapped out and finally admitted my total submission.

The fight for my life was on, and strangely enough, I felt up to it!

Get Busy Living!

- What are you running from?

- What are you afraid to admit?

- What are you trying to hide?

- What part of your outward appearance are you working hardest to maintain and protect?

- What part of the image you project is real and what is compensating for some inadequacy inside of you?

- What would you most like to run toward?

- Most men carefully guard an unexpressed **EXCEPT THAT** inside them. They already know what they could either start or stop doing that would radically change their life's trajectory. Turns out that most men will do anything **EXCEPT THAT** to heal or move on. Identify your **EXCEPT THAT** and you will be well on your way. Your **EXCEPT THAT** is the overgrown trailhead to your most profound inner work.

CHAPTER 15

Finding My Way Home

> "Faith is having one foot on the ground, one foot in the air, and a queasy feeling in your stomach."
>
> —RITA RIZZO

Some men unconsciously wish to get back home on the inside, but many continue to hold out hope for a simpler geographical cure. If they change jobs, the ache might go away. Maybe if they swap out their wives for a new one, the internal pain will subside. Perhaps they have just been living in the wrong ZIP Codes. They think that things will improve once they switch neighborhoods.

Trying to change the world around us to help us feel better is usually a cloaked strategy to avoid hard and transformative work.

Unfortunately, geographical cures don't work. They don't minimize the pain; they often multiply it. These strategies might work if we could leave ourselves behind in our maneuvers in and out of towns. For good or bad, wherever we go, there we are! Amazingly, we forget that we are the only humans who will never leave us.

I remember being bored as a kid. I recall feeling like there were 186 days in the month of July. There were three options we had to occupy ourselves in those long summer months: 1) Tennis ball baseball in the cul-de-sac, 2) Playing Kick the Can, and 3) Running through the sprinkler.

I promise I know what good old-fashioned boredom feels like. If I am honest, I kind of miss that feeling.

In the winter months, we'd play Atari Pong for hours and had each other convinced that no future electronic gaming system could ever be cooler. For my brothers and me, when Atari released the joystick, it was as if man had discovered fire for the second time. Boredom now had a new adversary. The Four Horsemen stalking the monotony of our days were named Asteroids, Missile Command, Centipede, and Pac-Man.

But being bored back then gave me time to think and dream. It built pressure inside to imagine and create. When I was bored, I naturally and inevitably wanted to do more and become more as well. Boredom is a great motivator if we let it instruct us. I didn't respect boredom or draw from it as much as I could have in my youth.

Instead, as a kid, I would find one of my parents and whine, "There is nothing to do!" or, "I'm bored, what should I do?" Both complaints assumed that keeping me entertained was their problem. In my laziness, I wanted to make them responsible for the lack of excitement in my life.

Consequently, I developed a bad habit of believing that someone else was responsible for keeping me interested and engaged. This was an early misstep and marked my inadvertently delegating this all-too important and private responsibility. It was an imperceptible shift, but it would eventually morph into my inability to answer the question that mattered most.

I never really asked myself this question before, at least not with any seriousness or depth. I abdicated and came to rely on others to define my life's bullseye. No one could give me the formula for success, but I learned the formula for failure—numb out to what makes your heart come alive; give up on your dreams! You'd probably agree, getting lost while traveling is a challenge we rarely run into these days, thanks to global positioning systems.

But I vividly remember my dad using a *Rand McNally Atlas* whenever we traveled. He probably felt like he had arrived when he joined the American Automobile Association (AAA). He hated getting lost. He would order an AAA "TripTik" every time he traveled more than 500 miles from home. These bygone relics were mini spiral-bound maps specifically designed for you and your upcoming trip, highlighting your route page by page.

Later in life, my generation graduated to MapQuest. We would print out accurate directions whenever we were traveling for business or pleasure. We would merely input the starting address and the ending address into their site and *voila*—we printed our step-by-step directions.

Just in case, many men held in reserve the Hail Mary pass. If ever in complete desperation and low on gas, they could always stop and ask for directions. It was an unspoken rule that this was for emergency use only, to be used as a complete and utter last resort.

What do you want?

Just like solving our boredom, something very important was lost on the way to making travel so darned easy. Most humans have lost the all-important sense of getting lost and then found. When the mind builds mental pictures and then operates on those imagined images, important synapses are developed in our brains. These neuropathways are vital for conceptual processing. They literally help get us from Point A to Point B.

And that works in the mental world as well.

Getting lost was something I got really good at when I was younger and not just because my older brothers were always telling me to get lost. Today, the average teenager can't get across town without their smartphones. Many of my son's friends willfully admit to being geographically illiterate without their iPhones. They are mostly unable to find themselves in space or to identify the four points on a compass. If I ask one of them to point to the south while standing in our yard, nine out of ten can't do it.

I recall being lost in Chicago in the eighties. It was my first time in the Windy City, and I was unfamiliar with their elevated train system, but I was young and overconfident in my sense of direction. Ten minutes later, my friend and I exited the "El" at what we had hoped would be the Navy Pier. Instead, we were at 74th Street, about twenty blocks away. We were officially lost, and both of us felt out of place and mildly vulnerable. I swear the overhead tracks looked just like the chase scene from *The French Connection*. With boatloads of good fortune, we hightailed it back to the station. Out of breath, we were able to catch the next train out. I had assumed I was bulletproof until I knew I wasn't.

In conquering the highways and byways, a big part of our personal resourcefulness was bred out of us. Being caught off guard in tight spots in foreign places had forced me many times to figure things out in a good way. I sensed my personal nimbleness expanding after I regrouped and got myself back on track.

Be honest with yourself: When was the last time you felt lost while driving somewhere? Better yet, can you recall stopping anywhere in the past five years to ask for directions? The map technology and the GPS functions built into our cars and phones are pretty much always accurate. We are so enamored with technological advances that we don't know what we have lost.

And it's altogether more terrifying to be lost in life.

There are no app stores or global positioning systems for that. Once you admit to going AWOL at some point in your life, the well-worn tools you reach for to stay on top don't serve you.

The return to the true you is a grind. There are no shortcuts. There's no GPS mapping specific to you. You can't use my map because my way back was unique. There are common directional

Finding My Way Home

cues and best practices too, but each map back is largely "one and done."

I mentioned the movie *The Bourne Identity* in an earlier chapter. Special agent Jason Bourne is a killing machine. His high-pressure training and an emotionally disturbing assassination attempt fried his mental circuitry. He struggles through the trilogy, trying to recover from psychogenic amnesia—a mysterious malady that erases his autobiographical memory. After hours of action-packed drama, he finally survives his almost-fatal identity crisis.

Watching these movies, I readily identify with the torment and hopelessness Bourne feels as he tries to piece together the disjointed clips of his past. Images flash randomly across his consciousness and painfully flood back, one frame at a time.

Not knowing critical information about myself freaked me out too. I began to feel like I was going crazy. My soul was doubled over with spiritual dry heaves for almost two years. It felt like I might have been at the end of myself.

Like Jason Bourne, I was also surrounded by good people who told me to be patient with the process. These incredible individuals assured me countless times that I would find my way back to the person I was meant to be.

In the middle of my life, I worked tirelessly in my mind to synchronize my past and present. It was as if I was playing a mental slot machine, hour by hour. I kept pulling the arm of my own one-armed bandit, and it kept coming up lemons.

My epic journey started in earnest when I decided to *come home*. Living on the run was no longer possible. Although it protects us from our pasts, it no longer feels sustainable. Faking it just becomes too painful.

The intensity of effort required to align my insides and outsides far outweighed anything I had done previously in my life. I was a human boomerang with a forty-year hang time. My life force, despite turbulence and strong headwinds, was finally headed back to my own front door.

Travelers on these personal pilgrimages admit that coming

home again feels like equal parts art and science. Exploration, investigation, and imagination are important ingredients as well. We have to get comfortable being uncomfortable.

My own journey was a weird mash-up of frustration, broken dreams, failed attempts to launch, tears, pain, the faces of my wife and children rooting for me, time alone in silence, exhaustion, profound loss, faith, chaos, my sister asking me what I was most afraid of, and my close friend challenging me with, "WHAT DO YOU WANT?"

In fact, it was that question that had remained stuck in my throat all those years. I was choking on it without even knowing. I longed for home in parts known only to me.

Others tried to talk me out of it. But there was no turning back.

Pain was the line of breadcrumbs that my life left for me. I recognize now that I had never intended to leave the real me behind. Going AWOL was my first singular act of trusting myself. In retrospect, had I not gone AWOL I might have imploded.

When I realized the heroism, I began to view the younger me as strong and tough as nails rather than weak and powerless.

The younger me was the hero, not the zero.

At about that same time, I realized my life had a game clock. I had been playing as if I had an endless shot clock, with ample time to become the real me. "When we get the family reared, get the kids through college, when my children get married to good humans, after we pay off our mortgage"—who was I kidding? Turns out, everybody but me.

At a low point, I remember receiving a powerful illustrated story of a man swinging on a trapeze.

Letting Go!

A man feels like his life is just an endless back and forth on the same boring trapeze bars with two or three simple releases and catches from time to time. He is lulled into a false sense of security, and he mistakenly believes he's in control.

But once in a while, he looks into the distance and sees a different trapeze bar swinging toward him. It's empty and looks both mysterious and dangerous. He knows that it has his name on it.

He hopes that he won't have to let go of his trusted bar completely. Maybe he can just extend himself, like Stretch Armstrong, to grab the new one. But who is he kidding?

He is filled with terror; afraid he'll be crushed if he falls. But he knows that holding onto the old bar is no longer an option. The new bar calls to him. So, he closes his eyes tight and hurdles across the void in between.

He finds out that it's in the transfer between the two bars where a supercharged life actually happens—that his time in flight was sacred, incredibly rich, and fertile.

He decides to hang out in the transition zone as long as he can to determine what it will teach him. *(Adapted, unknown source).*

Pain and faith had coaxed me into having both feet off the ground. Astonishingly, the familiar queasy feeling in my stomach wasn't nausea, it was excitement.

It turns out that hurtling through that void is the only space where human beings learn how to fly.

I anticipated my return to the sacred place inside that I had left behind, and I felt energy crackling inside as I came back to life. I closed my eyes and breathed into myself a gentle reminder to leave the front light on, because I was finally on my way home and this time it was in earnest.

Get Busy Living!

- Don't stay stuck where you are. The most alive you feel is when you are off the trapeze and hurtling through the air.

- Go for it. No matter where you are in your life's journey, time is fleeting.

- Live like you are dying—because you are!

- Don't just sit there, do something!
  Don't just do something, sit there!
  Which strategy hurts more? Do that one!

- Start by doing one push-up, start by writing one page, start by writing one letter, start by telling one person you are sorry, start by sitting in silence for ten minutes, start by walking for thirty minutes twice a week with your wife, start by turning your phone off, start by trusting yourself, start by writing one affirmation on a Post-it Note. . . and stick it where you can see it. Start being kind to yourself and believing in a rich and abundant future. Start today. **Repeat tomorrow.**

CHAPTER 16

The Dysfunction Stops with Me

"As a veterinarian, I rarely meet
a person with a dog problem;
but I meet six or seven dogs a day
with real-life people problems."

—PARKE "BUD" JOHNSTON, D.V.M.

It is hard to admit when we have a problem. Unconsciously, we project our issues outside of us and wait for the world around us to change. We want everyone else to transform without having to shed our own dysfunctions. It's a fact: The world around us won't change until we do.

Getting a solid grasp on our pasts won't kill us. Instead, it will inform our conscious minds and unlock the creative energy that has been in hibernation, held prisoner by the limited images we held of ourselves.

We are the only ones who know when we unplugged our important parts that need to be plugged back in. Admittedly, that restoration can be complicated. We don't want to give away hard-fought gains that now make up the virtuous and authentic parts of us. Take comfort in knowing that shedding your mask merely reveals what has been hidden from your own view all along. The worst fallout of wearing the mask—fooling ourselves—can finally be behind us.

It may sound like I am urging you to pull the drain plug on who you have worked so hard to become. That in a split second, you risk being reduced to a shallow puddle of the resilient person you have fought so hard to craft and develop.

Many men feel that looking back is too dangerous.

I get the concern, but it's not true. It comes down to how sustainable you think your current effort is over the long haul. How willing are you to work like a dog to accumulate more of the stuff that hasn't worked yet? Do you think 10-50 percent more of your current results gets you to a happy place?

I see it more like the younger me and the adult me huddling up and colluding for my ultimate rescue.

Zack, a former colleague of mine, has earned the right to boast of the epic account of his own return and rescue. Both of Zack's parents were profoundly bipolar. By early elementary school, he knew there was something dreadfully wrong with his mom and dad. Zack's mom was his father's third wife, and she had also been married previously. Throughout their adult lives, neither of his parents were able to hold a real job for any significant amount of time.

By the time Zack was in the fifth grade, his father had gotten caught up on the wrong side of organized crime. While at dinner one evening with some hooligans, he was drugged and left for dead. As if they hadn't done enough damage already, they stole his car.

Miraculously, Zack's father survived. Barely conscious and without a car, he staggered home in the dark of night. On a desolate highway overpass, he was again struck by the same mafiosos who doped him earlier. They ran over him with his own stolen car and left him for dead a second time at the bottom of a steep embankment. Hours later, he bear-crawled back home nearly broken in two.

By the time he woke up the next morning, he looked like

The Dysfunction Stops with Me

he had gone a hundred rounds with Apollo Creed. He barely recovered and was never the same again.

Zack's mom and dad later divorced. His mother eventually remarried for the third time. Zack's dad remained forever unavailable and self-absorbed and died alone and estranged from anyone who might have cared.

We make choices, then our choices make us.

In high school, Zack became utterly resourceful out of pure necessity. He believed from that point forward that his future would depend completely on his own efforts. He wouldn't depend on others; they would only let him down.

One night, as he and his stepfather argued over his curfew, things became heated. The man stood up and slapped Zack across the face. After that, it didn't go well. Zack pounced and quickly bested his stepfather.

Before the man knew what had happened, Zack was on top of him, choking him to death. At his mother's urging, he let his stepfather go and left the house, reminding him that Zack's mother had just saved his life. "Next time you touch me, it will be better for you to be in a plane crash!" were Zack's final words before peeling out of the driveway.

Fast forward a year later, his mother's depression worsened, and she was admitted to a mental hospital where she underwent electric shock therapy to jumpstart her brain into a better state. His mother eventually returned home, but it wasn't long before she succumbed to her life-long illness. Sitting in the barn with her Corvette running, she took her own life. The loss was devastating for Zack.

It is NEVER the right time to be an orphan.

A few months after his mother's funeral, Zack was locked out of his childhood home by his stepfather. Twenty years old and wondering if he had any more tricks up his sleeve, Zack shifted gears into full-on survival mode. His stepfather countered, true to his character, by disowning him and keeping all of the proceeds from his mother's estate for himself.

Zack's life is the stuff of movie scripts. To know him today is to love and admire the man he has become. He not only bested his stepfather that day, but he has also beat the dealer, making the most of the unfair hand he had been dealt.

Dogged persistence, personal rigor, and white-hot desire became Zack's greatest allies. His success was not overnight.

He reminds his own family each day that grit and determination come from surviving hardships. His personal mantra since college has been, "The dysfunction stops with me!"

Zack didn't run from his past, cover it up, or hide from it. He faced it and made getting in front of it his own heroic challenge. He vowed to overcome it and not to subject his wife and kids to the same chaos.

He is open about what happened and shares his story openly when helpful or appropriate. He is proof that our pasts have the power to either confine or refine us. They can fuel us in remarkable ways if we let them.

We are only as sick as the things we keep in the dark.

Another friend, Dan, is someone I look up to a great deal. He is unlike anyone I have ever met. More than anyone I know, Dan has made the journey back to his authentic self. He spent the early years of his life trying to outrun what he thought was true about himself. His life illustrates how putting your greatest fear out there for others to see can free a man from the hidden bondage of wearing a mask.

Dan describes himself as a "Mob-Dog." This is an overly amped-up version of a used car salesman. He spent most of his professional career in the manufactured housing industry—a more respectable term used to rebrand what many referred to as

The Dysfunction Stops with Me

"mobile homes" or just "trailers." He got his start in construction by pouring concrete pads in trailer parks and quickly decided he would devote his career to improving the perception of an industry that had nowhere to go, but up.

In the early years of his adult life, Dan wrestled hard to hide the true image he held of himself. Behind his workaholic, successful exterior, he felt like he didn't fit in, no matter who he was with. He had always felt different. He felt "goofy" compared to more polished peers. He wore Coke bottle glasses and was never very athletic.

Ever since grade school, he had been fascinated by the people around him and would join in conversations, hoping his questions would help him better understand what drove their behaviors and positive outcomes. As a matter of self-defense, he wanted to know what made people tick, unaware that it would have been better to turn his curiosity inward.

Fear of being rejected haunted Dan in his alone time. So, he kept himself ultra-busy and laser-focused on becoming outwardly successful. He eventually discovered that wealth and money were primitive ways to get a thumbs-up from the culture. His material success was an unseasoned feast; it filled him up but didn't taste very good.

The trouble with success and wealth is that, like Beowulf's sword, they evaporate when you are fighting to reset the image you hold of yourself. Money, no matter the amount, can't transform the fraction inside you into a whole number. Remember, multiplied fractions don't get bigger; they get smaller. Money and outward success will *never* get your internal numerators and denominators to match!

As Dan's business grew, he began to work with various media outlets. He used television advertising for his high-end mobile and modular homes. He wanted to sell to people who had never viewed home ownership as an attainable goal, but his early attempts in TV advertising were a complete flop.

Distraught, he and his team developed a new media strategy.

The result was like those Reese's Peanut Butter Cup commercials, where someone eating a chocolate bar runs into someone else with an open jar of peanut butter to create a unique and wonderful combination. Dan decided he would put his greatest fear out there for everyone to see.

Keep in mind that Dan's greatest fear in life was that people would view him as goofy, odd, out of the ordinary, and that he would be rejected. So, his scriptwriter came up with an idea for Dan to dress up in an almost skin-tight red leotard and prance around affixing, "Dan, Dan, The Red Tag Man" price-reduced tags to his inventory of manufactured homes. Among other things, he called himself "The Red Tag Man." He played the quirky double-wide superhero perfectly, and the public responded in a big way. Sales doubled year over year for nearly two decades.

His greatest perceived weakness became his superpower in business and in his personal life as well. He put his "goofiness" out there for everyone to see. He was out on a limb. It scared the heck out of him, but he learned to live out there and loved it.

And like the Reese's ads, something magical happened: His greatest fear lost its death grip on him. He has spent the rest of his career dipping from his own deep and clear well of inner confidence. Its source is the peaceful, easy feeling that comes from being known and accepted by his own audience of one.

What are you afraid of?

If we are ever going to adequately fill our internal vacancy, we need to thoughtfully revisit the instances that disconnected us on our insides. Depending on our life experiences, this will likely be some of the most important work we do as adults. Looking for creative ways to get the nonsense (stuff that now makes no sense) up and on the outside of us might be terrifying. Yet fear gradually gives way to curiosity and the thirst for greater insight into what has shaped us.

Until recently, only a few people knew that my greatest fear

The Dysfunction Stops with Me

was spending my entire adult life being bullied. Like Marty McFly in the movie *Back to the Future*, I was convinced I was destined to spend the balance of my adulthood shining a variety of "Biff's" cars and hoping they'd give me occasional "atta boys" for jobs well done.

Right about the time my dad knocked me off balance deep down, a kid from my grade school started bullying me. I mentioned previously that I was used to getting bullied by my older brothers, but this bullying was different. Something about being off my home turf gave this dude a greater advantage over me.

If you go back and check my attendance record at school, you will see I missed an awful lot of Mondays. I would lie awake most Sunday nights during my fifth and sixth grade years envisioning new ways he would humiliate me. My outsides were sounding the alarm, but no adult was listening. It was not the fear of him physically that scared me. Rather, it was this idea of being humiliated that kept me up at night.

I continued to grow physically, and the boy eventually stopped harassing me. Maybe he figured that he'd better not wake a sleeping giant. In my freshman year of wrestling, I saw him weighing in as one of the lighter weights on the opposing team. I remember asking myself why I ever let him bully me. I never listened for the answer until much later in life.

Not knowing what was fueling this, I let myself get pushed around, which meant bullies kept showing up in various ways. Dogs smell fear; turns out, so do bullies. It was time for me to face the past and unlearn the lessons that I had uploaded from my grade school experiences. Pain was my perpetual teacher. It invited me to its classroom time and again, but I had consistently RSVP'd *"No!"*

I let myself be bullied because that is what I thought I deserved. We teach people how to treat us. For many of us, now is the perfect time to fire the instructor who has been teaching our "how to treat me" class. Thank him for his good intentions, but make it clear that his services will no longer be needed—

effective immediately!

Pain finally came for me in the most profound way. On my knees, I was finally ready to process what had happened to me. I knew it was time to face the consequences of betraying myself.

What road are you on? Where is it taking you?

It was almost twenty years ago. I was coming to consciousness after receiving an hour-long rub down from a professional massage therapist. I am not sure what motivated this good woman and friend to do so, but she wrote the following on a piece of scratch paper and handed it to me on the way out of the appointment. I have read it innumerable times since. The original penciled message in cursive has blurred. Now, it's yours.

"DUH"
I went down a road and fell into a ditch.
I went back down that same road, I saw the ditch, but still fell into it.
I went down the same road again, saw the same ditch.
I tried my hardest; I gave it my all, but still fell in.
Duh, I needed to find a different road!

In my twenties, I toyed with buying a motorcycle. A wise friend convinced me to take a motorcycle safety class first. Motorcycles were provided as part of the class. The sessions were held four Saturday mornings in a row. The coursework taught basic motorcycle safety to help new riders avoid injuries and fatalities.

Besides convincing me *not* to buy a motorcycle, the course taught me something valuable that I will never forget.

On the final day of the course, the instructors lined up an exhaustive course of large orange pilons for each rider to navigate. The route twisted and turned several times and even doubled back on itself. We were told to hit as few of the cones as possible. The twelve riders lined up, and we took our turns.

Fortunately, the cones were heavy-duty because they were run over during all twelve runs.

After our first set of trial runs, the instructors immediately regrouped the riders. They reminded us to focus on the space between the cones, not on the cones themselves. We were told that if you look at the cone, you hit the cone. That had a profound impact on my next ride and became an important set point for other parts of my life as well.

What we focus on...becomes!

The body follows the mind. As a youngster, I wish I had known that my mind's focus leads and the rest of me follows. The concept gets better! It turns out that we are all hard-wired in our brains to help make day-to-day navigation more unconscious. Informed by earlier experiences imprinted on us when we were young, we locked ourselves in on a destination and set off to reach it.

If our future is going to be different from our past, we have to make different choices. Shockingly, discipline and personal rigor take the backseat in the reshaping of our lives. These virtues are not the dominant force that fuels or foils our rebuild. There is something far more persistent and inventive that we unwittingly disabled the moment we went AWOL.

Imagine that each of us has an intangible black box inside. This device functions much like a master recorder deep in our unconscious mind.

This is where we record what we believe about ourselves at a very young age. This imprint persistently follows us into our futures. It silently, but convincingly, informs us of what to think, say, do, and experience.

These pre-programmed coordinates drive a large percentage of our daily choices and behaviors. Our black box can lift us to great heights or keep us from ever taking flight.

But what if we choose to reprogram our own black boxes?

Since we were vulnerable and immature, we often drew faulty and damaging conclusions about ourselves when we first skipped out on our "real McCoy." Our black boxes were initially programmed with bad data.

The messaging is different for each of us, but the impact is universal and hugely significant, almost too big to calculate: Our lives become a perfect reflection of the image we hold of ourselves in our subconscious.

Do you think it is about time to find your black box and dub over the recording you have been listening to?

None of the stories, insights, or self-discoveries that I have related here matter in the least unless they draw you into the narrative of your own life.

Knowing when and how you prematurely abandoned your own self is your ticket out of the place that no longer serves you or your family. Replenished and fortified from the inside, you will be better than you ever imagined.

I hope this book has banged a drum that resonates with your own "Inner Knower." I hope it turns up the volume on the small voice inside that is beckoning you back to your frontline. I hope my word pictures have provided some much-needed encouragement for your journey home.

The voice might start small and distant. You may even scoff at it at first, but if you give it your time and attention, it will gradually stir the needed resources within you.

In time, you will get your feet back under you enough to stand up to whatever ensnares you. With joy and anticipation, you will hear yourself exclaim with confidence and renewed resolve, "Let's go!"

This is my enduring hope for you:

Gladly, with unrestrained elation, you will greet yourself arriving at your own front door. Without words, you will understand and nod, forgiving yourself for leaving in the first place. You will thank yourself for being brave and courageous, and you will praise God Almighty that you found your way back to the place you started from.

Get Busy Living!

- Stop giving a rip about what others think about you. Get serious about living your best, most authentic life.

- Wouldn't it be good to know what imprinted your life and is impacting you for good or bad today?

- Look at your life and consider that it is a perfect reflection of what you believe is true about yourself.

- If you think the problem is "out there," *that* is the problem.

- Choose your pain: Hurt now or hurt a whole bunch more later.

- Pass it back or pass it on.

- Become a professional at living your own life.

Conclusion

"Too many of us are tiptoeing through life, hoping to reach death safely. Instead, we should be praying, 'If we wake before we die.'"
—EARL NIGHTENGALE

Have you ever been frustrated trying to get some small appliance to work, only to discover it wasn't plugged in? I have.

I always feel like such an amateur when this happens. Afterward, it seems so obvious. I am surprised that I can still miss looking for the more obvious causes of things not working. Sometimes I think we have been trained to believe that the more complex something is, the better.

I have felt this way in my life's journey as well. I spent far too long being unplugged from my source of power and creativity. The reason was so obvious; I just didn't think it could be so simple.

In this process of reclaiming our lives, we must be careful, or we can believe we have wasted a big chunk of time that we will never get back. We need to recast our pasts as the upper-level classes we took toward securing a PhD in our own lives.

Looking back, we will see the perfect timing of it all and recognize the brilliance of the script we have been co-writing with the Creator.

This past summer, I read Matthew McConaughey's biography. I loved one short story he told about a monk he met while visiting a monastery in New Mexico. McConaughey wanted to talk to someone about his past and was wisely directed to Brother

Christian. The two went on a long hike and McConaughey bared his soul, making a fearless list of all the things he had done in his life that he regretted. Br. Christian said nothing, just listened empathetically.

For McConaughey, the experience must have been horrifying and humbling. At the end of the hike and his exhaustive confession, he turned to Br. Christian and braced himself for a long list of "could haves" and "should haves" from the holy man.

Instead, Br. Christian simply said, "Me too!"

McConaughey slipped right off the hook. The voice that had made him feel like he was the only one who would have done those things was silently sequestered. How great is that?

Regrettably, we hold tight to all our "take it to the grave" stuff, only to find out later that our mistakes are neither terribly awful nor unique. Most of the things we regret are common parts of the masculine journey. This is not an excuse for being selfish or self-centered, but a good explanation.

In 2002, I met my own version of Br. Christian in Chicagoland. Father Max had been conducting retreats for high school students for thirty years, and more than 150 high school boys and girls participated in his spiritual retreats each year.

On the final night of the three-day program, Fr. Max would ask the kids to consider the toughest trials which they had experienced up to that point in their lives. He wanted them to identify the one burden from which they would most want to be free; the one thing they each did or had done to them, that they wished they could undo.

He would then ask each individual to write that thing down, anonymously, on a piece of paper. On the last evening of the retreat, Fr. Max turned all the lights down except one lamp on a makeshift desk at the front of the room. He told the group that if they were okay with it, he was going to read each of these heaviest burdens aloud—no names, of course.

Everyone agreed, despite being unsure where it would end up. Before starting, he encouraged them to listen intently and try

Conclusion

to choose one of the other students' burdens that they would exchange for their own.

Over the thirty-year span, more than 4,500 students attended these retreats. In all those retreat experiences, there was never a single person who was willing to trade their unique burden for someone else's. Each burden seemed to be uniquely suited for each individual.

I'd say 4,500 kids is a statistically significant sample. Have you considered that what you are holding on to is actually the footbridge back to the most important part of you? Could it be the key that was fashioned just for you? Is your legitimate life experience the truth that you have been seeking all these years?

It's easy to forget that my ultimate purpose is to be me. It's not more complicated than that. When I take responsibility to live my life, that solitary decision takes everyone else off the hook.

Being ourselves is the place we all want to move back to.

When you come to love and accept yourself and your past, your external search gets refined. You are no longer looking to catch yourself in your past doing something wrong; you become more curious and less judgmental.

If we do this "Return to Me" thing right, we can finally see that what we thought were flaws were actually parts of our purposes—like the boy who resented being shorter than the other kids in school before he became a jockey and won the Triple Crown. With good fortune, we come into ourselves and see the careful knitting involved in all our life experiences.

Of all the men I have done life with, my friend Kurt's life story might top them all. Early in our friendship, it took the good part of three hours for me to get through listening to just a portion of his life story. Several times, I found my eyes moistened and my throat constricted. Twice, I was actually crying.

Kurt is just like you and me in some ways. But when you meet him, you will immediately sense something very different about him, in the best way possible. When Kurt talks, he isn't just saying something, he has something to say. He has been to hell and back a few times. He bought the t-shirt and subsequently outgrew it.

The uber-condensed version of his life:

Kurt was a drug user for most of high school and college years. He graduated with a minor in recreational drugs.

As an adult, he became addicted to crack cocaine, and his affliction of smoking it three to four times a week lasted nearly ten years.

Amid all the drug abuse, he was also posing as a husband and father. Incredibly, he was still broadly viewed as a trusted thought leader in his local commercial construction community. He was freakishly talented and equally tormented. Like many men, he overestimated his ability to pose and outrun the damaging things that hunted him. Kurt hurt everyone he claimed to love.

To do Kurt's story justice, I would need 10,000 more words just to scratch the surface. He was in and out of rehab countless times. Wherever he went, dumpster fires broke out in his life and the lives of others.

Because of this, his full recovery is miraculous and inspiring. His willingness to bless others with the striking details of his story is breathtaking. He wasn't just telling me; he was telling everybody.

When he and I reached the end of his story, he asked me, "Do you know what I love most about my life?"

I guessed that what he loved most was that his life was restored, or that his business was vibrant and well-respected, or that his marriage was intact and thriving, or that his kids still loved him and were actively pursuing their own dreams.

Surely, one of those miracles would top his gratitude list.

But no. He told me he was most thankful for being a "crackhead" in recovery.

He assured me that all of the good things in his life, all the things that people loved about him most would not have

Conclusion

been possible had it not been for recovery as a washed-up and hopeless crack addict.

Today, he is pursuing the hearts of lost and broken men while running a well-respected architectural firm. What he used to think was a curse is actually the thing he loves most about himself as a human.

In a recent video, Kurt relayed, "If you removed my past from my story, you would remove 90 percent of what is effective in my life. I experience profound miracles almost daily, and if you eliminated addiction from my story, I'd be a pretty impotent human being."

His life was surrendered on the outside but only because it was finally true on the inside as well.

As part of writing *AWOL*, I shared review copies with fifteen people, mainly family and close friends, before submitting to my editor. I wanted to be sure that what I was writing made sense and didn't seem self-centered or boastful.

After reading it, my good friend, Marty, asked, "TD, how do you know when you are no longer AWOL?"

It was a great question. It ricocheted around inside of me. I didn't want to be too quick with my answer, I wanted my response to be genuine and on point.

A few days later, I texted him the following:

"When you know with absolute certainty that you wouldn't trade your life for anyone else's; that you wouldn't risk changing a thing about your past because, in doing so, you'd forfeit the chance to be you and to love your life."

I added, "When you can say this and mean it, then you lay claim to being certifiably no longer AWOL. You get to spend the rest of your life being Bad Ass You and that gives you a reason to feel truly free on the inside and out."

Afterword

"Even a blind man knows when he is in the presence of a bright light."
—HELEN KELLER

A number of years back, I was on a four-day silent retreat at the legendary Gethsemane Monastery in Bardstown, Kentucky. When I arrived, there was spotty cell service, so I took this as a sign that I should leave my cell phone in the car. After all, I went to immerse myself in silence, and electronics can distract even the most committed pilgrim. So, I dropped it in my glovebox and made my way to the Monastery.

Three days into it, I broke down in the early afternoon and went out to my car for a quick reconnection with my world back home. I mostly just missed my wife and kids and craved a quick jolt of Vitamin D.

I retrieved the phone. Darn it—there was still no cell service. I wandered around in the surrounding meadows and hilltops, in ever-widening circles. I prayed I'd connect with the nearest satellite. After about three minutes, my phone rang. Bingo! I had service!

It was an unknown number, but my immediate impulse was to answer.

I said hello and was surprised to hear the voice of a relatively new, but already close friend, Eric. The first day I'd met Eric at church, he'd reached his hand out for a shake and said, "Hi, I am Eric, and I have stage four pancreatic cancer."

I learned a terminal illness resets your game clock and dispels any need for chit-chat. This phone call from Eric was urgent and candid.

"TD, I just left the oncologist's office. There is nothing left for them to do. I just have a little time left. I want to make the most of my last look around."

I wasn't ready for this. Who would be?

He went on. "I was wondering if you would be willing to walk out the last part of my life with me?"

I'd like to blame my reaction on not being in the right state of mind, but that would be too generous. In my immaturity, I quipped, "Before I say yes, Eric, what does *walk this out* look like?"

He shot back, "I don't know, TD, I've never died before!"

Stunned and chastened by his wit, I said, "Yes, I'd be honored."

After hanging up, I recalled something a famous person once said: "I am not afraid of death; I just don't want to be there when it happens!"

Nothing gets us right to the point like pain.

Through the next six months, I learned so much about Eric as he wrestled with his own demons of self-doubt and regret. I realized that, for most of my own life, I had feared death. More accurately, I feared my own mortality. It's a small nuance, but to me, the concepts are very different. Death is an event, a point in time; my mortality is more haunting and persistently bangs on my conscious mind.

Mortality challenges me to stay aware and plugged in, knowing that there is still time left on my clock. It challenges me to consider if I am listening to or ignoring the voice deep inside, my Inner Knower. It wants to know whether I intend to make the most of the time I have left.

That summer, Eric and I logged many hours on the journey toward the end of his physical being. There were high points and low points along the way. The one that sticks out most, besides the moment he took his last breath, was a story he told me about a lunch he had the month before he died.

Afterword

He called to say he had just left Noce's, a small New York-style pizza parlor where you can buy an authentic slice of pie right out of the oven. He said, "The weirdest thing happened to me at lunch." While he was waiting for his pizza, he noticed an older man across the room.

He thought to himself, "Man, that guy is one handsome dude. When my slice arrives, I am going to stop over at his table and ask if I can sit with him for lunch. I'd like to get to know him." He admitted this sounded more than a little crazy.

As his pizza arrived, he mustered the nerve and approached the guy. In an instant, he was overcome with emotion. He recognized that the man he had intended to have lunch with was actually his own image being reflected to him in the mirror from across the room.

Talk about greeting yourself at your own front door!

Like you, perhaps, I didn't believe this story at first.

I wondered if Eric had dreamed it up or, worse, made it up. However, the more he and I leaned into it, the more convinced I was that it actually happened as he told it.

What a great place to land just before you die. To finally hold yourself in such positive regard that you feel attracted to and want to learn more about the man you are and the man you dream to be.

But we don't have to wait until the end of our lives. We can get after it now. It's about time you get after finding yourself, don't you think?

Eric's story provides just one more poignant and well-lived example of how it feels to return from being AWOL. All these true stories from men should beckon each of us back toward that person inside; the one that we left far too long ago.

That AWOL part of you is waiting patiently as well, trusting that you haven't forgotten him and knowing you will make the journey back to your own front door.

The still-small voice is warning you to not tiptoe through your life; after all, what point is there in reaching death safely?

Field Notes

Field Notes

Field Notes

Field Notes

Field Notes

Field Notes

Provisions for Your Journey

It would be unfair if what I have written in AWOL leads you to believe that recovering a connection with your younger self is easy. Reclaiming the important and lost aspects of you is a process, not an event. In this endeavor, some people are going to think you are crazy. Like the two guys who free-climbed the Dawn Wall route of El Capitan, your sanity may be questioned. You will likely hear your effort is either too dangerous or impossible. When you decide to make this trek, you are sure to experience fear, confusion, uncertainty, and dread. Climbing interior mountains is like that. It takes truckloads of tenacity and trust.

Going in is ultimately a willingness to sacrifice, surrender, trust, and transform. You cannot change, and at the same time, stay as you are!

The following list of disciplines, exercises, and resources helped me in my journey back to the forgotten parts of me. There are surely other tools that you might stumble upon to help fortify and sustain you. Please view each outlined here as time-tested beacons and buoys.

If you get a moment, let me know how your journey unfolds.

Fitness and Wellness

I believe one of the easiest ways to support your recovery is to take better care of your body. Nurturing your physical well-being has a nearly immediate impact on your psyche. Improving your physical experience by making the investment in eating better and exercising has multiple rewards. Keep it simple, and develop a plan today that gets you moving in the right direction.

Fasting

It is an embarrassment of riches, but in most first-world countries, people eat constantly. We have become grazers, and the amount of great tasting food always within an arm's reach presents a real challenge for getting and staying fit. There is so much good content out there outlining the benefits of setting specific eating windows in which you fuel and nourish your body. See if fasting can help you reset your relationship with food.

Personal Budget

Understanding your relationship to money is super helpful as you make your way back to your home base. How we handle money speaks volumes about what we value most. But living within your means can be the financial equivalent of eating right and exercising. It can be easier said than done. Maybe find someone who is really good at this part of life and ask them for help and guidance. Get over the initial embarrassment and dig into it. Your financial mentor will be flattered, and you will get to chart a financial future that is much different from your past.

Minimalism

It is fair to say that we have too much stuff. Minimalism is a movement that is slowly catching on. Decluttering our physical space also helps free our minds and hearts. A thought leader in this growing trend, Joshua Becker says, "Minimalism is the intentional promotion of the things we value most and the removal of anything that distracts us from it." I am convinced that this has enormous benefits in multiple areas of our lives.

Mentors

There are tons of people further along in their journeys than you are. These folks would love to help and can provide you with a real positive lift in your journey. My bet is that when you do your own about-face, capable people will just start showing up. Take them up on their offers to help. Remember, the theme song in hell is, "I did it my way!"

Find Five Bad Asses

Someone I look up to a ton credits his ongoing success in personal development to curating a short list of five exceptional individuals who are on his speed dial. He knows that he becomes like the men he hangs around. To qualify, each of these guys must be serious about life and their own recovery. My buddy's list evolves over time. If someone drops the ball and goes off-reservation, then he puts that guy on waivers and picks up a new draft pick. Sounds harsh, but he knows the inescapable impact these individuals have on his life.

Nature and Adventure

This one is often overlooked. We have become chained to technology and the comforts of home. Getting out in the woods reconnects the ignition switch to our soul. Our minds get clearer, and our imaginations are recharged. In nature, our pulse quickens, and we get back in touch with the cosmic wonder of being human, of being fully alive. Go to your nearest REI store and ask yourself how you can plug into activities like hiking, mountain biking, skiing, kayaking, or camping. You'd be surprised how much energy you can recover inside yourself, by spending an afternoon landscaping in your backyard.

Meaningful Work

Many men are leading lives of quiet desperation. We spend more time at work than at any other activity besides sleeping. Don't settle for just making a living. We can't all be astronauts, but we needn't settle for some humdrum existence in our work, either. If you haven't yet, restart this part of your journey with more self-knowledge. Take the *Myers-Briggs Type Indicator*, discover your strengths with the *StrengthsFinder*, assess your dominant work-related traits with the *Culture Index*, or take time to learn about the *Enneagram*. Behind knowledge of God, knowledge of self is the next best one to acquire. The more you know about yourself, the more you will know about what brings you to life.

Movies

Movies can be game changers. They engage with our imaginations and our senses too. They are super-sticky, and their themes inspire us and stay with us. Watch *Good Will Hunting, Shawshank Redemption, The Greatest Showman, Cinderella Man, Gladiator, Rocky* and *The Count of Monte Cristo* and see what happens. The movies we love touch the parts of us that want to be activated.

Music

Music transports us; lyrics capture parts of us that remain unnamed. Songs remind us of the common parts of our human experience. We resonate with music. If movies are sticky, then songs are like super glue. Music shapes culture—there is no denying this. Music shapes us as individuals, too. What we listen to infuses us; we become what captures our imaginations.

Stories

I can recite word-for-word the stories that have changed my life. Stories can realign what we previously thought possible. Once the four-minute mile was broken, within the next week, several other men followed suit. Just knowing that it could be done gave others permission to break through to new levels in their own performance. What stories are you listening to that help you shatter barriers? What stories are you telling yourself? Immerse yourself in the power of good stories and watch them change your life.

Books

Books about personal development have had a deep impact on my life. We all experience books differently. They can be great launching pads in our journey to reset how we show up in important areas of life. We may read many books, but classic books read us.

Creating

Make something. Whether it be in the garage, the yard, your basement, the kitchen, or on your doodle pad. Get yourself back into the mode of making something, even if just for the fun of it. Heck, if you don't know where to start, get a coloring book and a box of crayons. Creating and expressing yourself can get you back in touch with the parts of you that are stuck or buried.

Rest and Relaxation

My goodness, could two words be more foreign to us, despite being English? I am not sure that some guys could define the words if pressed. Get familiar with the word "margin" and seek to add it back into your life in generous measures. You have proven to yourself that what gets scheduled gets done. Start scheduling time to unplug. Make "Bel Far Niente" your weekend battle cry ("beautifully doing nothing").

Family Time

If you can, spend time with your parents, siblings, and other close relatives. You will be amazed at what memories come back to you. Pay attention to what you remember and ask yourself how those experiences inform and shape you now in your adult life. Adults are kids in big clothes. We came by our emotional habits honestly. Have the guts to sign up for the classes that get you the PhD in your past!

Old Photos

There may be no better way *in* than taking *out* the photos from your early days of being a kid. If you sit with them for any meaningful amount of time, your memory will flood, and your senses will activate. You will recall what it felt like to be you and get back in touch with the things you loved about your childhood and the things you left covered up. Both are important parts of your story.

Imagination, Visualization, and Meditation

All of these important tools are performed in the mind. Our minds are incredibly powerful. Everything that we create is formed twice, once in our minds and then in its material form. Use your mind to recreate the imprints of your life experience. Leverage your imagination to activate a counter force to the parts of you that sabotage and tether you to unwanted outcomes. There is a much better way; you just haven't *seen* it yet.

Therapy

Having somebody who knows the way in and agrees to stay close by you as you unpack your past is invaluable. They provide powerful commentary and insight from an unbiased perspective. They re-witness the parts of your past that have formed you and can make powerful connections that you might have passed over. Naturally, we can also make snap-value judgments about our past behaviors. More than anything else, these pros can be both ally and advocate in our recovery. Two important individuals, in two different therapeutic tours, helped flip my view of my younger self from Zero to Hero.

Journaling

This one is a go-to for many who rely on the written word to express themselves. Using thought prompts can better access the conversation that is going on inside your head. The chatter that can seem like a nonsensical babble oftentimes makes perfect sense when filtered into the written word. Over time, your journals stack up and become trusted resources for your ongoing journey.

Spiritual Direction

Good spiritual discernment is hard to come by. In my honest opinion, God gets far too much credit for the bad things that happen to us and far too little credit for all the good that comes our way. Discerning what is a prompt from *The Hand That Writes All*, as opposed to the result of a bad burrito and a terrible night's sleep, is key.

Faith community

There is something very attractive about being with people who are also making a spiritual journey. Not feeling alone in the massive undertaking of building my faith muscles stabilizes me and pumps belief and resolve into my soul.

Giving and Receiving Love

There is nothing riskier than love. What you commit to loving will decide everything. To love well is to consent to walking through life with your heart on the outside of your body. Recommit to being real; read *The Velveteen Rabbit*. Ask yourself if being real is worth the risk.

Solitude and Silence

This is a two-step process. Solitude is being alone; silence frees your mind from distractions that otherwise block out the noise that clamors around on your insides. The more you befriend both disciplines, the more comfort you gain from being in your own skin. Solitude and silence are the foothills from which a great spiritual life ascends.

God

The moment you believe you understand God, you do not. He exists outside of time and space. He is in and above everything; He is both source and summit. When we don't know where to turn, that's when God is closest. With no need for our acknowledgment, God provides the escape velocity needed to overcome the gravitational force that keeps us attached to the dysfunction of our past. We can easily forget that God isn't mad at us; He is mad ABOUT us!

Acknowledgements

I feel as though I have been standing on great people's shoulders my entire life. My friends are the only trophies I have kept; outside of my wife and kids, they embody the best "wins" of my life.

I am forever grateful to Tom & Judy Dierker, Dave Dierker, Barb Weaver, Mark Dierker, Shell Laumer, Tim Dierker, Bill Dierker, Joe Dierker, Mary Elizabeth Weaver, Sierra Laumer, Alaina Laumer, Jack & Ellen McFadden, Luke Franer, Liz Franer, Roger & Theresa Baldwin, Mary Miller, Nancy Smith, Paul Borgman, Dick Klus, Sandy Davis, Tom Meyer, Carl Hauck, John Hussong, Lloyd Dissinger, Larry Sunderhaus, Dan Klare, Mike & Gayle McCafferty, Pat Hudepohl, Roger & Nancy Johannigman, Randy Freking, Jeff Betz, Paul Hemmer, Sr., Paul & Joeline Lecture, Fr. Mark Burger, Jim Telles, Scott Heisel, Dave Datillo, Fr. Tim Howe, Mike Luerhmann, Tom Young, Mike Zicka, Braden Mechley, Betsy Hendy, Rob Daumeyer, Craig Todd, Trey Rouse, Brad Arling, Rick Fehr, Dave Foster, Steve Ramos, Fr. Matt Gamber, Matthew Kelly, Dr. Ron & Carole Good, Dr. Bob and Lisa Good, Gina Romano, Sam Ferroni, Fr. Bob Sherry, Walter Solch, Ray Nickel,

AWOL

Julie Gomez-MacLean, Mallary Washbish, Bud Johnston,

Mike Momper, Jeff Miller, Dr. Bret Bruder, Jim & Barb Momper,

Jim & Joan Gardner, Fr. Ron Rieder, Jan Zalla, Peter Bronson,

Jim Schmitt, Bob Schmitt, Ken & Marcia Schibi, Fr. Jim Willig,

TD Hughes, Mike Snell, Mike & Wendy Lundberg, Mike Rumage,

Doug Harris, Mitch Smith, Mike Monahan, Steve Sester,

Christy Wheeler-Geha, Paul Ziegler, Cara Croley, Tim Miller,

Bob Koenig, Gale Banta, Bill Dermody, Neville Brown,

Rocky Kalsow, Ken Robertson, Jay Lieser, Larry Axt,

Craig Sullivan, Craig Corbett, David Heidrich, Scott Millay,

Marty Boyer, Matt Daniels, Julia Ayala Montes, Alex Perez,

Dr. Robert Caldemeyer, Fr. Baiju Kidaagen, Jeremy Armbruster,

Laurie Groseclose, Dave Kampsen, Dan Ruh, Dave Neyer,

Dan Rolfes, Mike Hardig, Mike Karman, Rick Schiller,

Merrill Hutchinson, Tony & Cheri Griffin, Fr. Michael Hennigen,

Tony Dressman, Tony Ward, Rick Lohre, Gary Kathman,

Matt Bischoff, Joe Hunt, Tom Ruberg, Mike Franxman,

Eric Miller, Rosemary Obrien, Brian Bozeman, Magic Marker,

George Josten, Eric Robbins, Tom Lipsey, Fr. Bob Sherry,

Jeff Coleman, Dave Haughey, Brian Sand, Sean Herron,

Alex Yungvirt, Joe Porter, Thomas Ziegler, Amy Tewes,

Maggie Pfeifer, Marcus Gardner, Jeremy Hill, Dave Whelan,

Alan Forbes, Fred Robbins, Brian Dunham, Leigh Hensley,

Acknowledgements

Joel Kubala, James Lenhoff, Charlie Hall, Kent Wellington, Patrick Reynolds, Chris Lewis, Andy Barton, Marcus Thompson, Kevin Rains, Brian Arlinghaus, Peter Kelly, Dr. Peter Ganshirt, Joe Fribourg, Pepper Sweeney, Sarah Schaefer, Mary Beth Wilker, Andrew Curran, Br. Luke Armour, Ken Berry, Derek Vanover, Fr. Bill Murphy, Erik Zimmerman, John Geisen, Josh Lillis, Jason Martin, Fr. Ethan Moore, Dr. Dan Fagel, Amy Lesniac, Dr. Steve Hamilton, Jim Tucker, Dr. Lynn Pierson, Luke Good, Zack Good, Stephen Andros, Kurt Platte, Jeff Smoker, Nick Wilmhoff, Todd Detering and Madison Hoehn for their guidance, faithfulness, and encouragement.

Dear Reader,

Mental Health and Wellness is a serious matter.

If at any point, you feel you need help, reach out to professionals or health service organizations. These folks can help significantly to guide you along your path.

If you don't know where to turn, local churches and faith groups can be a good place to start. Asking a close friend that is well-grounded is also super helpful and can be less intimidating.

Either way, do not underestimate the seriousness of the inward journey. Sure, it is sobering and at times challenging, but it's likely that you have what it takes to do the work. I trust you will come out a way better you on the other side of all your efforts.

Sincerely,
TD Dierker

CHAPTER 13

The Pain That Comes for You

"The pain will leave once it has finished teaching you."

—UNKNOWN

For me, the way back from being AWOL was tougher than I could have imagined. I had to retrain my brain. Reprogramming a thirty-year narrative is nearly enough to break a man!

My return to becoming more real would sadly be an arduous process, not a simple event. There were countless false starts, and my authenticity and discipline ran hot and cold.

There are several types of hurt to contend with in life. As I have grown older, I have experienced pain in a variety of ways. Joy has shaped me too, no doubt, but pain has sanded me down in more memorable ways.

Regret and disappointment plagued me in my young adulthood. I walked away from darn near every serious challenge I faced. False starts and no-shows were the story of my youth. In the early going, I was hoping that the way out for me was as easy as deciding to reinvent myself. Unconsciously, I think I was counting on being afforded a massive do-over in my early twenties. I would just call "Ollie, Ollie Oxen Free" or "Uncle" to myself, and others would allow me to get back safely to my invisible internal base.

After making a massive reset from the man I was to the man I intended to be, I thought I would be in the clear and able to run wide open toward how I wanted to express my life. If only life played fair and let me call my own plays and run them successfully.

The start of my rebuild was like watching a complicated in-air refueling of a large jet airplane. Both the fighter jet and the refueling jet were moving through space; any good result would rely on a steady hand, keen expertise, and mostly guts. My first attempts were "no bueno!" I wanted to hit the ejection button a few times and abort my mission.

I was desperate to eliminate the fear and pain; I never considered that I was meant to learn from them.

I now know that the fear and anxiety that I experienced were sent to teach me something valuable. They were trying hard to get my attention and to alert me to how much was at stake. I never really grasped this until much later in life. It would have been ludicrous at the time for me to believe the pain was some sort of benevolent instructor. If someone would have suggested that to me, I would have told them to buzz off, STAT.

Most days, it left me feeling disoriented. I was sure its intent was to ruin me; therefore, I was hell-bent to eliminate it. The pain spooked me. It felt random; I couldn't tie it directly to a clear trigger. I would never sit still long enough for a meaningful dialogue because it had me running. I was afraid of my own fear.

In my case, I thought that carving out a more virtuous exterior life was my best solution. It would at least stop the external bleeding. I didn't pay enough attention to know that the internal hemorrhaging raged on. If I did notice, I likely punted on it by telling myself that I would deal with the inner stuff later.

The Pain That Comes for You

Meanwhile, I was still trying to stuff the holes in my soul with the affirmations of others. Like an addict who becomes resistant to lower doses, as I grew older in years, I needed more affirmation and validation. My fragile sense of self was rising and falling mostly on the opinion of others. My boss' impression of me could change the atmosphere inside me within a nanosecond.

Now is yesterday's later.

I have worked hard in my career from my early twenties to my mid-fifties and have had several professional successes. Ann Marie and I very much invest in our marriage and work hard to actively love each other. We have tried our hardest to stay awake and alive enough to not knowingly wound our seven kids. Time will tell if we have been successful.

I have invested heavily in my personal and professional relationships. To the untrained eye, it seemed as though I had a tiger by the tail and had done a great job of training it to obey my commands. But that was a stark contrast to the reality of my inner life.

Inside, I equated my self-worth with my professional success. Interestingly, I always worked directly for the founders or presidents of organizations that employed me. I have been counted on as a rainmaker and change agent in all of my positions since graduating from college.

I have thrived in these competitive environments, and I've enjoyed moving things from Point A in a steep ascent to Point B. As a highly paid performer, I was transfixed by both the clock and the scoreboard. Not surprisingly, so were the men to whom I reported.

But that resulted in a very subjective view of my performance and left a whole lot up to the interpretations of the person who was paying me. It became increasingly hard for me to judge my own performance. I felt like an Olympic gymnast, forever focused on turning in a top performance so that I could win over my curmudgeonly Russian coach. My validation came from outside of me. As a result, all the fun had been drained out of my professional existence. I became excessively identified with and defined by the reflection I was getting in cheap mirrors held by others. Over time, the crazy-making funhouse of other people's opinions of me had become no fun.

At times, I felt like a guy flying an F-16, diving from dizzying heights on risky missions. All the while, someone else could eject me from the cockpit at any moment.

No matter what you do, performing while trying not to lose is a bad recipe for a high-quality life.

I resisted politicking and padding my nest at work, so I spent very little time actively managing individual perceptions. I always maintained the belief that good eventually wins, so this emboldened me to trust my intuition to take risks. This all sounds really good, right? You might even resonate with some of the confidence and chutzpah in my approach to work.

But I spent most of my career vacillating between being an esteemed fighter pilot and wondering if I even knew how to put on my flight suit.

Looking back, I am overcome by the realization that I was setting up my professional life to mimic my third-grade experiences with my dad and brothers.

Unconsciously, I had recreated those early relationships near-perfectly; likely trying to recast the opinion I had formed of myself on the inside.

I recall a wise priest telling me, "If one man calls you a jackass, dismiss the accusation. If a second man calls you a jackass, consider it. If a third man calls you a jackass, then you had better start looking for a saddle!" I was brutally aware that I was the common denominator in all the dysfunction.

I have held only five posts in my work life. Each had weirdly similar roles, even though all five competed in dissimilar industries and market segments. Remarkably, as if I were being drawn by some unseen force that wanted to replay the events of my